A NEW LOOK AT
THE APOSTLES' CREED

A new look at

The Apostles' Creed

Edited by
GERHARD REIN

AUGSBURG PUBLISHING HOUSE
MINNEAPOLIS · MINNESOTA

Copyright © 1969 Augsburg Publishing House
Second Printing 1977
All rights reserved

Library of Congress Catalog Card No. 72-75401
International Standard Book No. 0-8066-0915-X

This book is a translation of *Das Glaubensbekenntnis*, edited by Gerhard Rein, published in 1967 by Kreuz-Verlag, Stuttgart, Germany

TRANSLATED BY DAVID LeFORT

Manufactured in the United States of America

PREFACE

In Letters and Papers from Prison, Dietrich Bonhoeffer wrote twenty-five years ago that we are being driven back to the beginning of our understanding in order to make the truth of our Christian faith comprehensible in the society around us which has come of age.

We are reminded of this sentence when we have read through the fifteen contributions on the Apostles' Creed by thirteen theologians and two laymen: eight of whom are Protestants and seven Roman Catholics. In this book, the contributors do not present a joint compilation with a systematic explanation of the apostolic confession of faith. This was not the intention. Each article stands on its own and each writer is only responsible for his own essay. Yet, they present aspects and reflections for a contemporary understanding of the Apostles' Creed which contains so many sentences and, again and again, presents considerable difficulties to open-minded and interested Christians—irrespective of their confession.

The series of the South German Radio, presented here in print, was entitled "In Defence of Thinking": because many Christians have forgotten that understanding and belief belong together. Those who take the Apostles' Creed seriously cannot thoughtlessly repeat it with the congregation during a service. We have to be able to think and reflect about it.

The writers in this book considered how today they could explain and understand the phrase which they were given, phrases which were defined nearly two thousand years ago. The discussions of the themes were developed by almost every writer in two directions: on the one hand the question arises as to whether or not and to what extent each section of the

Creed was authentic, and thereafter how it could be made feasible to contemporary readers. With great freedom, they begin from the point that the Creed, even from the start, was interpreting the biblical tradition and that it therefore can and must be interpreted further. Conformity to the written words of the Creed is not a question of their verbal confirmation of biblical history but it is a question of the relevant, applicable and expounded statement of each section. The writers do not attempt to construct a continuity of salvation history between the individual sections. This cannot be done. The individual parts of the Creed were put together once but now only the various sections can be continually spelt out—an extending constructive effort.

The contributions taken together will show that the statements concerning who God is and how he affects men, are not unreasonable. They touch much more on the being of God orientated towards the basic question upon which the life of man hangs or falls. "Open-mindedness, a readiness to enquire and a preparedness to enter into the darkness of fear," and the author concludes, "I believe that it is better to cast away one's self-concern, to take risks, to sacrifice oneself in order to be able to find a final comprehensive understanding, rather than expound to oneself nothing but empty talk—taking refuge behind defused verbal ammunition." As long as such basic questions are put, consideration of what is in the Apostles' Creed, such indicated stages and positions of the history of God's dealings with men is meaningful.

GERHARD REIN

CONTENTS

	page
Preface	5

WALTHER VON LOEWENICH
Origin and Significance of the Apostles' Creed .. 9

WOLFHART PANNENBERG
I believe in God the Father Almighty 14

HEIMO DOLCH
Maker of heaven and earth 20

KARL RAHNER
And in Jesus Christ His only Son our Lord .. 25

GERHARD GLOEGE
Who was conceived by the Holy Ghost, Born of the Virgin Mary 29

HEINRICH SCHLIER
Suffered under Pontius Pilate, Was crucified, dead, and buried 34

JÜRGEN MOLTMANN
He descended into hell 39

GÜNTHER BORNKAMM
The third day He rose again from the dead .. 45

ANTON VÖGTLE
He ascended into heaven 51

HANS CONZELMANN
 And sitteth on the right hand of God the Father Almighty; From thence He shall come to judge the quick and the dead   57

WALTER DIRKS
 I believe in the Holy Ghost   62

ALBERT VAN DEN HEUVEL
 The holy Catholic (Christian) Church, The Communion of Saints   67

MAX-PAUL ENGELMEIER
 The Forgiveness of sins   73

MAX SECKLER
 The Resurrection of the body   78

GERHARD EBELING
 And the Life everlasting   82

WALTHER VON LOEWENICH

Origin and Significance of the Apostles' Creed

It is worth while to devote a series of lectures to the explanation of the so-called Apostles' Creed, for this creed is still the most widely accepted summary of the content of Christian belief. To this day it is recited in common at most evangelical religious services, and most Christians have known it by heart from childhood. The Apostles' Creed occupies the second chapter of Luther's Small Catechism which, despite the many difficulties it presents for untrained minds, is still the most widely used "Theology for the Laity" in Lutheran Germany.

Luther regarded the Apostles' Creed very highly because he felt that it was an excellent brief statement of scriptural doctrine. In a sermon in 1535 he remarked, "Neither we nor the early fathers invented this confession of faith, but just as a bee collects honey from all kinds of beautiful flowers so is the Apostles' Creed a finely constructed summary of the whole of Scripture, the writings of the beloved prophets and apostles, for the benefit of children and simple Christians." For Luther, the Apostles' Creed is simply "the faith." This is why he often commented upon it and included it in both of his catechisms.

For the Reformation the Apostles' Creed was also of great importance, because it was one of the three major creeds which linked Christianity to the early church. Today we would characterize this function with the word "ecumenical." The Reformation did not intend to be looked upon as a sect, but as a renewal of the one, true, and catholic church. This is why the reformers, while stressing their own confessional formulas, maintained the three ecumenical creeds of Western Christianity as the basis of faith. The other two creeds are the Nicene and the Athanasian. The former is the creed of the

Council of Constantinople in 381 and is *the* creed for the Eastern Church, which uses neither the Apostles' Creed nor the Athanasian. The Nicene Creed marked the end of the Arian debates in the fourth century, as may be seen from the additions it contains compared with the Apostles' Creed. The Nicene Creed appears in the Roman Mass, though with an addition about the Holy Spirit that is unacceptable to the Eastern Church. The Athanasian is a purely Western creed. Strictly speaking, none of the three creeds is wholly ecumenical, though the word may be used to characterize the principal content of the Apostles' and the Nicene creeds. The Apostles' Creed is used in the Roman breviary and may be generally considered as a bond of unity among the Christian confessions.

The Apostles' Creed therefore has an important significance for the church. In the church's struggle for existence during the Third Reich, many Christian communities became aware of this. Their common confession of faith became a genuine profession of the essential points attacked by public authority. We ought never to forget this in our changed situation today.

For there is no denying it: there exist generally serious doubts as to whether the ancient formulas of the Apostles' Creed are still capable of giving adequate expression to our contemporary belief. The famous Luther expert Karl Holl wrote in 1919: "At the present time no one among the theologians or among the faithful is able to accept the Apostles' Creed any longer in its precise meaning." Surprisingly enough, such opinions had already been voiced in the seventeenth century, the age of Lutheran orthodoxy. At that time the theologian Calixt proposed the Apostles' Creed as the basis for union with the Roman Church, inasmuch as this creed contained a full and clear statement of all the truths important for salvation. Calixt's orthodox antagonists violently opposed this thesis, for the creed does not contain the doctrines, so decisive for the Reformation, of original sin and justification. Luther's commentary gives to the Apostles' Creed a deeper significance than originally present, so that identical confessional formulas do not necessarily mean identical confessions. Doubts about the adequacy of the Apostles' Creed grew apace with the Enlightenment and with the advances in historical-critical research in the nineteenth and twentieth centuries.

To support his politics of Prussian unification, Friedrich Wilhelm III ordered a more extensive liturgical use of the Creed, and the new Lutheran orthodoxy of the nineteenth century made it a binding doctrine. This really caused the theological opposition to increase. A notorious "battle of the Apostles' Creed" resulted from the refusal in 1891 of the Württemburg pastor C. Schrempf to recite the creed at baptisms. Harnack, pushed by his students, made a famous statement: "One shouldn't abolish the Apostles' Creed since there's nothing better to take its place; one simply has to reinterpret it." After World War I, disciplinary measures or suspensions were connected with the name of Leimback and Knote, while before that there were Jatho and Traub. The ecclesiastical authorities did not have a uniform standpoint, and the appointed disciplinary boards did their job with no easy conscience. Now and then the rules were relaxed.

Even now the situation is far from clear-cut. The conservative tendency has gained ground by way of the later Barth, and this has helped the position of the confessional formulas. But over against this, the most recent theological development has raised the question whether the confirmation of the objective facts of salvation as proposed in the Apostles' Creed is not in fundamental contradiction to the very essence of faith. People are demanding the demythologizing of such "objective" statements by way of an existential interpretation.

In any event, faith must be distinguished radically from the recognition of so-called historical events. This obviously has important consequences for one's attitude toward the Apostles' Creed. This is very closely connected to one's attitude toward Scripture itself. The Apostles' Creed is rightly so called inasmuch as it does reproduce the essentials of the apostolic faith, but the formulation does not, as once assumed, derive from the apostles themselves. Until the fifteenth century humanist Laurentius Valla denied its apostolic origin, it used to be thought that each of the apostles had contributed one of the twelve articles.

There are creedal formulas in the New Testament; especially important is the trinitarian baptismal commission of Matthew 28:19. This shows the origin of such confessions: the person to be baptized professes his faith. Later these confessions, with the necessary additions, served as a defence against heretics. This was the case for the Nicene Creed. In the early church there were quite a number of these confessions of faith; among them the most important for the Western Church became the Roman baptismal confession which probably goes back to the middle of the second century and even then contained many additions. It decisively influenced the formulation of the Western confessions of faith. The text of our present Apostles' Creed was witnessed to in Gaul and West Gothic Spain in the fifth century. At the time of Otto I it was introduced in Rome as the baptismal creed. Since then it has remained essentially unchanged and was taken over by the Reformation.

What meaning can such a creed have for us today? First of all, it indicates that the church is more than a group of purely subjective believers. The creedal affirmations refer back to the mighty deeds of God. They are not, in the first instance, expressions of religious feelings but records of events. The church is not founded on piety but on that which God did, and still does, for man. This is the significance of creedal objectivity.

At the same time, the creed is the bond which throughout the centuries has linked contemporary Christianity to its historical origins. This is the ecumenical significance of the creed. If the church were to divorce herself radically from this bond, she would be liable to the danger of disavowing Christianity itself.

At the same time, however, the objective creed ought to express our subjective confession, and this is the reason for the difficulty mentioned before. Can we demand that the scientifically trained theologian of today subscribe literally to the Apostles' Creed? Or will such a demand produce hypocrites? Is it not blasphemous dishonesty to have recited before the altar a creed to which we no longer fully subscribe? Perhaps the theologically trained pastor understands it quite differently than his parish. Perhaps among the parishioners the understanding varies greatly. One accepts it literally, another hesitates, a third interprets it in his own way. There are surely modern ways of interpreting it; but interpretation can lead to distortion and to dishonesty. The main thing is to be clear about what is actually meant.

Only one thing will avail: the laborious, patient education of theologian and layman in the correct and honest understanding of the truth of Scripture in obedience and freedom.

WOLFHART PANNENBERG

I believe in God the Father Almighty ...

Not too long ago most Christians took for granted the idea that there is a God the Father. They did not think that this first article of faith was something exclusively Christian, for they knew they held it in common with the majority of civilized people. Difficulties with the traditional creed began first with its statements about Christ as the Son of God and with the miracle of his birth and resurrection. Faith in Christ seemed a disturbing addition to the simple belief in God taught by Jesus himself. Today the situation is practically the opposite. There appears to be no room left in the world for a God; even theologians talk about his death. The only secure element in the Christian tradition seems to be Jesus with his message of love.

Some theologians do try to substitute faith in Jesus for faith in God. I think that anyone who proposes this does not really consider what it means to look at Jesus with Christian eyes. How can we believe in Jesus and commit ourselves unconditionally to him if he is just another man among men? To believe in Jesus and commit ourselves presupposes that he represents the reality meant by the word "God." The message of Jesus was in fact governed wholly by the idea of God and the nearness of his kingdom. Jesus' notion of love of neighbour was a consequence of his message about God and God's love for man. We have to admit that a crisis in our thinking about God places the future of Christian faith in danger.

What is meant by the "death of God"? It is an ambiguous formula, for it expresses an image rather than a specific thought. The image is that God once lived, but now he has died. But was a God who is no longer God ever really God? In this case the death of God is more the end of an *illusion* than of a real God. In this way, the "death of God" appears as the metaphysical expression of the discovery that man's ideas of God contain merely human dreams, mirror-images of man himself, and do not refer to any reality independent of man.

The notion of God's death did in fact arise principally from the disenchantment of religious consciousness. The spatial notion of God sitting on a heavenly throne was simply a metaphor even for ancient Christian theology. It meant that God was hidden, that he lived in a dimension of reality inaccessible to man's everyday experience. We can also say that God is the depth of reality, and this is a spatial image too, no different than the one about God in heaven. No medieval theologian would have been surprised upon hearing that the space ships of the twentieth century did not encounter God. The spatial image of God living in his heaven has long been recognized as a metaphor; this is not what has shaken the idea of God for modern man.

What is of much more influence is our inability to think of God as a purely spiritual being. As long as the human soul was thought to be fundamentally separate from the body so that it left the body on death, it was possible to look upon God in an analogous way as a bodiless, spiritual being. Precisely as bodiless, God had no need of a specific dwelling place such as heaven. But now that we can understand the soul only as a function of the body, so the conception of God as a purely spiritual being no longer means anything to us. And if this image of a divine spirit fails, there fails along with it the traditional notion of God as a person, according to the analogy of the human person and human self-consciousness. It is hardly possible any longer to maintain that the ideas of God as a spiritual being and as a self-conscious person are anything more than blown-up mirror-images of man. A hundred and fifty years of criticism have shaken the foundations of the traditional idea of God. But does this mean that we can no longer talk meaningfully about God? Or doesn't this crisis rather force us to a new and more profound approach to the mystery behind the word "God"?

One can also go in the opposite direction and try to explain the reality we experience without any reference to God. This is, after all, the experiment which humanity is engaged in today: to live without God. But is it successful? Has it succeeded? Isn't man's experience poorer, hasn't it lost a dimension, by excluding all talk of God?

The word "God" refers to the impenetrable depth in the being of man and world. Neither the variety nor the oneness in the diversity of reality is fully accounted for in our scientific knowledge. The mystery remains. It is not that we are still limited by a prescientific, primitive approach to reality, an approach which will be superseded through further scientific progress. No, the farther our knowledge advances, the stronger becomes our sense of the inexhaustibility of reality.

When we speak of God, we refer to the mystery of being not only as the background of finite things, for the word "God" means also that this mystery is met in its power in the events of human history. Most religions attribute a mysterious power to finite things—to the stars, for example. The Old Testament, on the contrary, distinguished the mysterious power from all things visible and saw its activity in the surprising, unexpected happenings of human history, an activity that could bring both destruction and salvation to man. It was above all the experience of unexpected salvation that founded Israel's faith in the mystery's goodness and mercy toward herself and all mankind.

Because the mystery encounters us in the concrete events of our life, we experience it as a *personal* power, and therefore as God. Here *person* is not analogous to the supposedly familiar nature of man. This very familiarity has made all talk of God trivial and unconvincing, a mere projection of the ideal man into an imaginary heaven. In this century, we have seen that our idea of the human person and its proper value is far from being taken for granted. It is, in fact, dependent on religious experience. The idea of man as a person and as inviolable is an echo of the encounter between man and the mystery which concerns him and grasps him and defines him.

It was first as a partner in the convenant with God, as one involved with God's majesty, that man was discovered as a person. Both the Greek and the Christian-biblical roots of our modern understanding of "person" have religious overtones. The Greeks looked upon man as a reasoning individual because he shared in the divine *logos* that governed the universe. In the Bible it is the teaching that man is the image of God that most approaches our modern notion of person. That man is destined to represent the presence and lordship of God in the world is the basis for the inviolability of the human person, the law against murder.

The contemporary idea of man as an "I" facing a "Thou" has its origin in the Christian doctrine of the Trinity. The "Thou" of the Father founds the "I" of the Son. The encounter with the divine mystery makes man aware of the mystery of his own existence. It is a puzzle how anyone could possibly arrive at the statement that man first had to consider himself as a person independent of any religious experience— as if there was any trace of a non-religious secularism before the nineteenth century—in order to then extrapolate the idea of person into the religious experience. This is contrary to everything we know of human history. First there came the experience of the personal character of the divine mystery. In Israel this was the recognition that the mysterious power that pervaded all of reality encountered man unexpectedly in the concrete events of history and made itself known in connection with earlier revelations, especially in its fidelity to a salvific will. Only because man became caught up in the mystery of divine power, only because of the covenant between God and man, did man become a person. In this differentiation and primacy of the personal character of the divine mystery in the face of whatever may be said about man as person and in the face of all anthropomorphic representations of God is the point of departure for a new and deeper insight into God's personal character to be found. In this way, our speaking of God will no longer be susceptible to the atheist criticism which is aimed at the human projections that are merely exaggerated mirror-images of man and human relations.

The early Christians who formulated the creedal confession of God the Father Almighty, did not labour under our difficulties. To speak of the mystery of being as personal and therefore as God was hardly a problem for ancient religion and philosophy. The problem then was to maintain the uniqueness of God in the face of the multiplicity of gods; this is no longer any problem for us today. If we accept at all the divine reality, we have nothing to object to its uniqueness and omnipotence. In this matter, we are the spiritual descendants of those who won the intellectual debates of that day. But we can possess our inheritance only if we are convinced of the personal character of our encounter with the mystery of being.

Does this mean that we can call God "Father"? The widespread use in antiquity of this name for the one or highest God is obviously bound up with the patriarchal structure of that society. In our day we would hardly choose "Father" to designate as person the divine mystery. But still, Father is not arbitrarily replaceable, for it identifies the personal God as the God of Jesus, as the God whom *Jesus* called Father. When we confess God the Father in the Apostles' Creed we do not mean that we have chosen what seems to us the most adequate name of God, but we mean that we confess the God of Jesus. And this is the God of Israel, whose almighty rule over the world is coming so that only in the future will his divinity be revealed, even though he now determines all that is now present in his hidden way.

This is why man cannot know this God without faith. One didn't have to believe in the gods of the Greeks because—for the Greeks—they were obviously *there*. But the God of Israel and of Jesus can be known only in faith because, in spite of all past and present experiences of his power and the comprehensive revelations of his divinity, the coming of his kingdom is still future.

The remaining articles of the Apostles' Creed explain the meaning of the divinity and rule of Jesus' God. They speak of nothing other than the God revealed in Jesus and present in his church. The articles on the Son and the Holy Spirit show who is the Father whom Jesus proclaimed. Perhaps for us they can shed light on the name of God the Father as the name of the God from whom we come if we inherit the Christian tradition, and who will reveal himself in his omnipotence in the future of our history, and who as Father will allow us to share in his life through his Spirit who raises the dead.

HEIMO DOLCH

Maker of heaven and earth . . .

In the Apostles' Creed the Christian acknowledges God as the Creator of heaven and earth. I want to show the significance of the acknowledgment by following up what W. Pannenberg said about the article "I believe in God the Father Almighty." I'll begin by singling out two points made by Pannenberg:

First of all, since Nietzsche there has been talk of the "death of God." According to Pannenberg, this appears to be "the metaphysical expression of the discovery that man's ideas of God contain merely human dreams, mirror-images of man himself, and do not refer to any reality independent of man." It arose "principally from the disenchantment of religious consciousness." It is a criticism of certain notions of God which grew up in the course of Christian tradition. Pannenberg remarks: "Isn't man's experience poorer, hasn't it lost a dimension, by excluding all talk of God? The word 'God' refers to the impenetrable depth in the being of man and world. Neither the variety nor the oneness in the diversity of reality is fully accounted for in our scientific knowledge. The mystery remains. It is not that we are still limited by a pre-scientific, primitive approach to reality, an approach which will be superseded through further scientific progress. No, the farther our knowledge advances, the stronger becomes our sense of the inexhaustibility of reality."

Secondly, I refer back to these words of Pannenberg: "When we speak of God, we refer to the mystery of being not only as the background of finite things, for the word 'God' means also that this mystery is met in its power in the events of human history. Most religions attribute a mysterious power to finite things—to the stars, for example. The Old Testament, on the contrary, distinguished the mysterious power from all things visible and saw its activity in the surprising, unexpected happenings of human history, an activity that could bring both destruction and salvation to man. It was above all the experience of unexpected salvation that founded Israel's faith in the mystery's goodness and mercy toward herself and all mankind."

We want to develop these thoughts of Pannenberg further here. As the Psalms indicate, the people of Israel kept asking themselves who this was that saved them beyond all understanding and who turned to them and all men in fatherly compassion and benevolence. The answer, incredible as it is to man, is that the one who saved Israel is he who shatters the cedars and makes the desert whirl. Behind these images of Psalm 29 lies the systematic doctrine of, for example, the second and much later story of creation from the first chapter of Genesis, the one who saves and rules Israel with mercy is not just another mighty one among all the mighty, but the absolute Lord of all, the Creator of all.

One meaning of the article of the Creed we are dealing with is that the Father is mighty in the sense of all-mighty. It clarifies the previous article: "I believe in God the Father Almighty." It prevents a too easy familiarity from sneaking into the Christian's thinking and speaking of God, as if God were the "dear God" with whom man easily stands on terms of equal footing. Of course, a Christian may and should say "Thou" to God, but the truth of faith that Jesus Christ has opened the believer's way to God the Father grows and thrives in its healthy form only from the ground on which Moses and the prophets of the ancient alliance stood: reverence and awe before the infinite majesty of God.

So, even without asking what "heaven and earth" mean outside of a general description of "all that is," there is a deep significance to this second article of faith.

We find another meaning to this article when we consider that there are such things as the North Star or the Milky Way. If we mean anything real and not just something mythological or legendary when we say that God is the Father of men, then we cannot call God the Father of the North Star. But are the stars and the nebulae, is the whole visible world which is subject to human research so worldly, as some people today would have it, that God has nothing to do with it? Our article of the Creed teaches us that there is nothing that escapes the relation to God; he is creator of all. Whether or not this total dependence of all things can be known by natural reason—this is yet another question beyond the scope of the creed.

The Christian believes that Jesus Christ became man for the salvation of men, that God's saving activity bears upon man. Whether it bears upon man only is a question often asked throughout the centuries; it is generally accepted that God's saving activity does have a cosmic dimension which reaches beyond man. Remember the thought of Teilhard de Chardin. All we want to say here is that not every work of God is for the sake of man. This does not mean that a world without men would be just as meaningful; it simply means that the universe does not depend for its meaning wholly upon man.

So we have found that the second article of the Apostles' Creed firstly clarifies the previous article "I believe in God the Father" and secondly guards against the always threatening anthropological reduction of God's revelation: God and his word are too rich to be limited to man and man's salvation—God embraces all. It is this article of faith that shows the insufficiency of describing God as the final goal of all human drives and that marks the limits of the so-called existential interpretation of Holy Scripture, whereby the Word of God has meaning only insofar as it means something for me.

But we can go a step farther. What do the words "heaven and earth" mean? What can "heaven" mean today?

It is well known that the ancients thought the universe was geocentric. In the centre stood the earth, usually imagined as a disk—beneath it the kingdom of the underworld and above that of the superworld, the heavens. Heaven was one of three possible domains. Copernicus laid this three-storied universe to rest. There is no longer a heaven in the ancient sense, but a space studied by astronomers and explored by rockets and astronauts. Is, therefore, all theological talk about heaven meaningless? It would be if that is all that the New Testament writers understood by the word "heaven." In the Lord's

Prayer we say "Thy will be done on earth as it is in heaven." It does not make much sense to pray that God's will be done where only the stars are moving according to unchangeable laws established by their Creator. The prayer means something only if, somewhere in the universe—in "heaven"—there are beings that not only "orbit" but that can act. And in Philippians, these words conclude the hymn to Christ: "in the name of Jesus, everyone should kneel, in heaven and on earth and in the underworld...." Here again we find the three domains, and here again it does not refer only to three possible geographical places. If it means anything, it means that somewhere—in "heaven"—there are intelligent beings who are capable of doing the will of the Father and of confessing the Christ. However impossible it may be for us to imagine what beings these may be, there should be little doubt of their existence, despite the current demythologizing of sacred Scripture. Sacred Scripture is God's Word for salvation or for condemnation, and how can we be sure when it saves and when it condemns? Couldn't it condemn us here if we leave out a text intended for our salvation? Is the writer of Philippians giving his own private opinion or is he transmitting God's Word when he says that our struggle is not primarily against flesh and blood (earthly powers) but against the powers of darkness? It is to make this clear that we have this last meaning of the article of faith: "I believe in the Maker of heaven and earth."

In the gradual formation of the Apostles' Creed in the ancient church we can see the following steps:

I believe in God the Father;

I believe in God the Father Almighty;

I believe in God the Father Almighty, Maker of all.

And this can be clarified in the phrase:

I believe in God the Father Almighty, Maker of all reality, visible and invisible.

Then, finally, came the expression: Maker of heaven (for the invisible reality) and earth (for the visible reality).

Without any doubt, it is more difficult for us today to imagine these powers than it was for men of the Baroque age to sculpt their angels. For us they are more anonymous and collective in nature. After the Nazi terror Satan may have lost his wings, but the satanic has shown itself to be very much of a reality.

As Yves Congar said recently: "When we call the church the *ecclesia militans* (the 'fighting church') this does not mean only that the faithful have to exert themselves now in order to enjoy the rest of Paradise. Much more, it means that the church wages a continual, dramatic war with the powers of darkness. No Christian can escape this 'spiritual' battle against the 'spirits' of evil, a truth too often passed over."

So the final meaning of this article of faith points to the history of salvation and to the following creedal statement about Jesus Christ the Saviour of man and the Perfector of every creature visible and invisible.

KARL RAHNER

And in Jesus Christ His only Son our Lord . . .

If one wants to talk religious and theological sense about Jesus Christ today, one must first describe the essence of *faith* as the act which looks to Jesus as the Christ. And when we speak of this faith in the first instance as event—and only consequently as content—then we presuppose that this faith is thereby more than a private and purely subjective affair, that it realizes itself within the *church* and in obedience to the expression of *her* "official" faith. This is the sense of a binding creed. With the church and in the faith of the church the man Jesus gives himself to men.

All this happens within the context of an absolute trust by which man surrenders himself to the other and thereby grasps in unconditional hope the right to success in every area of his being, which from the very nature of this total surrender he is unable to comprehend adequately. From his own point of view, that of absolute expropriation, man can call the one to whom he entrusts himself by various names: "Lord," "Son of God," "Forgiver," "Saviour," and a thousand other titles given him since New Testament times. It is thus a secondary (though important) problem to determine which of these aspects of total demand is the most adequate for furthering modern man's encounter with "him." Would it be better to speak within an apparently private perspective of the forgiveness of personal guilt or, within the context of universal history or cosmic evolution, to appeal to the meaningful end of history in the Omega of world evolution? The most different approaches are all doors to the radical self-surrender of the whole man to Jesus Christ, and this is their only significance.

This is not the place to discuss the question of what is involved in encountering the concrete man Jesus so that an act of total expropriation results. Although of decisive significance for the understanding of Christology and for our consideration here, it is is not possible to explain now why such a free act of trusting, hoping, and loving self-surrender in the face of the other includes, as the ground of the act, the knowledge, however unreflected it may be, and the acceptance of what we mean when we say "God." But presupposing this, we can say that whenever one entrusts himself *with reason absolutely* to another and whenever this other *in his own right* can accept this trust and is thereto empowered by God and by no one else, then this other man enjoys a unique and radical unity with God. And this unity is ultimately and rightly and radically explained by that which is confessed of Jesus in the orthodox Christian faith, however each individual may understand and explain his own experience of trust.

If we are honest, we have to admit to the men of today that the doctrine of God's incarnation sounds like pure mythology which no longer makes sense. But if we listen closely to the *genuine* teaching of the faith about the God-man, then we see that it is not demythologizing but only correct understanding which enables it to remain *wholly orthodox and yet credible.* When we use our own everyday language in saying that "God became man" then we automatically either think of a transformation of God into man or understand "man" in this context as a costume or puppet through which God represents himself on the stage of world history. Both of these are meaningless and just the opposite of what the Christian dogma really intends to say. For God remains God and does not change, and Jesus is a real, genuine, finite man who has experiences and who stands before God in reverence, a free and obedient man, like us in all respects.

What does this fundamental statement of Christian faith mean? From a dogmatic viewpoint, it is perfectly legitimate to maintain that a man who without further mediation and in his own right can assume for himself the act of absolute trust in God must enjoy a unique union with him. On the other hand, we can also say that this unity, the mystery of Jesus' sonship and incarnation, can be expressed in existential categories which describe the spiritual self-realization of man. Man exists as the derivative and the called, as he who answers yes or no in his derivation from and his tending toward the ineffable mystery we name God. This coming from and going toward are characteristic of the essence of the spiritual creature. The more radically these tendencies are fulfilled, the more independent and free is man. Their fulfilment is equally God's gift and man's act. Now when there is a man who receives his essence from God in this sense and directs it back to him in such absolute purity and so radically that this man becomes God's irrevocable message to the world making him present, then this is what we call "incarnation" in orthodox dogmatics. This teaching on the unity of the divine person and the two natures—divine and human—refers to the same mystery in ontic-substantial categories as may be described as well in existential concepts. The only condition for the mutual substitution of these expressions is the understanding that they really include one another.

We must understand that this man's act is the act of the God who constitutes this man. We must not look upon this relation between God and a man as a purely supplementary, peripheral "disposition" that leaves man untouched in his depth. It is only necessary to understand that God did not simply make man an open question pointing to God but that once he gave this question a possibility and a reality to answer itself unconditionally and fully and to assume therein God himself.

Faith's message about Jesus Christ is not a myth or a fairy tale. It proclaims the radically *singular* event of the accomplishment of the *final* possibility of the essence of man. Faith has the courage to accept Jesus of Nazareth as he who in obedience to the God-founded depth of his being has appropriated God, as he who was accepted as such (as shown by the resurrection), as he who *could* because he *was* and is ever accepted by God so that his life showed historically the reality he is: the self-expression of God to the world, irrevocable in and through its radical and divinely accomplished acceptance in the true man Jesus.

Whoever experiences in faith that he trusts Jesus of Nazareth *absolutely,* that in Jesus God gives himself unconditionally and irrevocably, that through Jesus one's own concrete encounter with a man in trust and love becomes absolute and *thus* is experienced what "God" means; whoever experiences this, I say, no matter how well or badly, however adequately or inadequately he explains it, believes in reality in what we Christians call the "incarnation," the unmixed and indivisible unity of God and man in which God remains God and man becomes wholly man and both are one unmixed and indivisible in Jesus, the Christ of faith. When we entrust ourselves to him radically, when we find ourselves before him alone, then we experience immediately *who* he is; our trust has its ground in that which he is. The circle cannot be broken. Whether one knows it or not, one draws God and man together. The Christian believes that in Jesus of Nazareth he finds both in one. This is the justification and ground of love towards all other men, and all such love is a way to that one man in whom the unity of God and man, intended for all, has found its singular historical expression and irrevocable finality: Jesus Christ.

The church rightly stresses the decisive value of her old Christological formula, arrived at after a long period of intensive thought. All other possible formulas have to be critically compared to it in order to guarantee that they maintain clearly and unequivocally that faith in Jesus recognizes in him not only a religious genius or the prophet of a passing phase in the evolution of religion but the absolute mediator of salvation, now and forever. Whoever accepts this in belief and trust makes real in his faith that which Christendom professes of Jesus of Nazareth, the crucified and risen one.

GERHARD GLOEGE

Who was conceived by the Holy Ghost, Born of the Virgin Mary ...

There is hardly a problem more impenetrable to modern thought than that contained in this article of the Creed. Even in the so-called "creedal struggle" in 1931, Adolf Harnack could say: "Here something is affirmed as a fact which does not allow a reinterpretation unless in the sense of its opposite. This leads to a crisis for every Christian who has to use the creed as an expression of his faith and yet cannot convince himself of the truth of this article."

One cannot satisfy the demands of thought by simply rejecting this judgment of their rationalistic grandfather. For more than a decade I led a student discussion group on this topic in Weimar. After several of the panel participants had taken the trouble of "defending" the article in question the students of natural science who were present explained that it wasn't worth the trouble any more. Modern biology has shown the reality of the propagation of lower forms of life by parthenogenesis. It is thus not unthinkable that, by way of exception, this fatherless procreation could occur on the human level. But besides the fact that such a limiting case has not been recorded anywhere, such recognition hardly serves faith. The ring of rationalism was not only broken but welded again, stronger than ever. What is the good of such reasoning? The twofold assertion about the miracle of Jesus' origin is referred back to faith.

But it is precisely before the tribunal of faith that this article is threatened more acutely than it could be by the most clever argument of reason. In a truly evangelical faith *what* is to be believed is determined in dialogue with the sacred Scriptures. But the New Testament hardly accords what is commonly assumed to be a central place to the statement "conceived by the Holy Ghost, Born of the Virgin Mary." It is not "necessary for salvation" that one assent to this statement. To be saved it is enough to look toward Jesus Christ who died for all men and whom God raised from the dead. If one asks about his origin, the New Testament answers unequivocally: It cannot be dated. As the "Word" of God, he *was* in the beginning with God (John 1:1). Paul cites an early hymn: He was "in the form of God, equal to God; yet he humbled himself to take on the form of a slave on earth" (Philippians 2). Still clearer is Galatians 4: "God sent his Son, born of a woman and subject to the law."

These Pauline sayings are of vital importance. They do, of course, use "mythological" language and reveal their meaning only to one who recognizes their unmistakable intention: to proclaim God's salvific will. This will is expressed in John 1:14: "The Word became flesh and dwelt among us," a verse which Schleiermacher recognized as the "basic text of dogmatic theology" and of "the whole ministry."

But both of these scriptural sayings, that of Paul concerning the Son who became man and that of John concerning the Word who became flesh, seem to exclude the notions of conception by the Spirit and birth of a virgin. Conception and birth cause someone to exist who never existed before, and yet the eternal Son, the eternal Word, "is" real eternally, just as God is eternally.

The task of faith is not easy. It has to make its truth accessible to the world. The "Good News" causes the faith to be creative. Luther called faith the "creator of divinity"—"not, of course, in the divine person, but in us." And in our case also, the faith was hard at work, not dreaming but wide awake, thinking, constructing. It's not a question of imagination let loose but rather of weaving the outline of the message in the fabric of earthly realities. Struck by the message, faith begins to report what happened when the Word became flesh. Primitive Christianity had no intention of recounting myths or fairy tales, but it did use the form of pious legend to emphasize the meaning of its message. There are only two places in the Gospel where this form is found: Matthew 1 and Luke 1—only here!

Matthew tells his story in eight short verses. Joseph wanted to leave his fiancée when he discovered her pregnancy, for he did not wish to accuse her before the law. An angel of God stopped him, however, by explaining that the child was conceived by the Holy Spirit and was destined to save his people from all their sins. All this had taken place in fulfilment of the Lord's promise in Isaiah 7:14: "Behold, a young woman is with child, and is about to bear a son; and she will call him 'Emmanuel,' which is 'God with us.' " Matthew ends his story with the report that the birth occurred.

There are two things to notice in this text. First of all, the story-teller is not at all interested in the miracle as such, but only in the fact that God has made good his ancient promise to send a Saviour for Israel. God did not lie: In Jesus, God entered Palestine. Secondly, the evangelist wanted above all to show that this event which entered the world "vertically" from above was the fulfilment of the "horizontal" history of Israel. This is why his report contains sixteen verses which record, in the form of a family tree, "the history of the Messiah Jesus, the son of David, the son of Abraham." Later tradition scarcely recognized the logical inconsistency of this added note with the original message of the incarnation of the Son.

St. Luke did not notice any inconsistency either. If he had, he could not have let his second chapter follow the first without any transition! The "shepherd story" in Chapter 2—our "Christmas Story"—mentions nothing about "conceived by the Spirit" or "born of a virgin." Mary is simply a young married woman who happens to be in a situation of earthly misery. She is not the centre of the story, but her *first* (!) son. Poor shepherds hear the news that this child in the manger is to save not only Israel but the whole world. In the "Mary story," on the other hand, an angel speaks to the Virgin Mary and announces to her the virginal conception. This is the slight textual basis for the later *dogma* of the virgin birth: a few verses of the first chapters of Matthew and Luke which seem to contradict not only the rest of the New Testament but even the very Gospels of Matthew and Luke themselves.

Did Matthew and Luke notice this contradiction? Obviously not. Why not? Because they regarded the birth of Jesus with completely different presuppositions than we have. We look for the "facts" in historical descriptions, the "accuracy" of reporting. For them what was reported was significant only to the extent that it gave a form that they could understand to the coming of the Son. They lived from the message that enkindled their faith: "Today is born unto you a Saviour" (Luke 2:11). With faith in the message they interpreted God's act in such a way as to make it significant for the Jewish and the Hellenist-Roman worlds of that day. They were neither asked for nor did they seek any documentary evidence. Matthew, for example, had such a narrow viewpoint that he did not even check the original text of Isaiah 7, which says that the Saviour is to be born of a "young woman." He was satisfied with the Greek Bible of the Jewish diaspora, which had changed the text from "young woman" to "virgin."

The infancy narratives, therefore, were governed by the Word of God as accomplished in Jesus Christ. Faith articulated its witness in legends. Its interpretation of a new world era was so realistic that it remained secure against any reduction into myth. The stories are very restrained. God is no Zeus who loves a woman and engenders the half-god Hercules. No description is given of the act of conception or of the actual birth. Both are secondary in comparison with the unique and fundamental occurrence: "He was revealed in flesh" (1 Timothy 3:16).

The "fact" intended by the twofold article is therefore to be understood as a *sign*. It testifies to the faith that "Jesus' birth was a creative act of God in a way that is not true of any other human birth: although Jesus comes within the framework of Adamitic humanity and shares its end (Romans 3:3), in his birth God becomes man and a new humanity begins" (Paul Althaus).

Before the court of reason this means that there is no question of erasing this statement of the virgin birth from the Christian creed, but of interpreting it on the basis of its fundamental intention. It is precisely its secondary value in man's eyes that allows it to guard the great mystery: man's lowliness is the form assumed by God's salvation. The Mary story underlines the fact that the future mother of Jesus is a lowly girl (Luke 1:38 and 46). Mary is no heavenly queen; as a servant, she submits to God's wishes. And, again, this shows that God respects the human body, as he allows his Son to become man. In the Te Deum, we sing: "You did not recoil from the womb of a virgin," or in Luther's version: "You have not disdained the virgin body to redeem the human race."

The Nicene Creed joins together the birth from the Father "before time and the world" with the "incarnation from the virgin Mary through the Holy Spirit." Luther in his hymn of faith connects the two so masterfully that the counterpoint of God's activity is easily heard: "We believe also in Jesus Christ his Son our Lord, who is eternally with the Father and like to God in power and reverence due, and who was born true man of the virgin through the Holy Spirit *in faith,* for us who were lost. . . ."

HEINRICH SCHLIER

Suffered under Pontius Pilate, Was crucified, dead, and buried . . .

If we listen closely to the Christological section of the Apostles' Creed, we are struck by the fact that so little is said of the events of Jesus' life. Besides his birth, death, resurrection, exaltation, and parousia, nothing else is mentioned in the Creed. The article we are now dealing with is a good example of this. From Jesus' birth we pass immediately to his death. Is there nothing else to profess about the life of Jesus Christ?

The Apostles' Creed is not the only profession of faith that takes a giant step through the life of Jesus. The old Roman Creed, for example, which was an earlier form of our Creed, manifests the same gap, at least as we've got it from Rufinus. And if we go farther back, we find the same in the anti-docetist creed of Ignatius of Antioch: "Jesus Christ who was truly born of the family of David, of Mary, and who ate and drank and who was truly persecuted under Pontius Pilate, and who was truly crucified and who died . . . and who was truly awakened from the dead." And in the background of the New Testament we find confessions of faith which refer to the same order of events and jump from birth to death or even from birth to resurrection. The famous hymn to Christ in the Epistle to the Philippians, which the apostle Paul took over from the primitive community and explained a bit in his letter, praises Christ's incarnation, his obedience unto death and his exaltation. And in the beginning of the Epistle to the Romans, Paul cites a brief profession of faith in the Son of God, "who was physically descended from David, and decisively declared Son of God in his holiness of spirit, by being raised from the dead." Here also there is mentioned only birth and exaltation.

No word is said of Jesus' earthly way and works in word and sign. This general consensus, from the primitive community up to the time of the Apostles' Creed, can hardly be a coincidence. There must be a basis in fact. If we clarify this, then we can better understand the significance of this article in the Creed: "Suffered under Pontius Pilate, Was crucified, dead, and buried."

We must recognize that Christological creedal formulas are not something like reports on the history of Jesus, for these formulas were formed by the Evangelists for the purposes of preaching from the tradition of Jesus' words and deeds. They are not a continuation of the Gospels, nor are they simply excerpts from them. Neither are these creedal formulas theological reflections that expose "the truth of the Gospel" (St. Paul) from a special point of view for the purpose of protecting it from misunderstanding, as we see in the letters of the New Testament. Our creeds presuppose the Gospel and apostolic reflection, but in themselves they are definitions of essences. These formulas seize upon the two events that reveal the essence of man, his beginning and his end, his origin and his destination, and conceptualize them. In this way they isolate, manifest, and safeguard the light by which Jesus, his person, and his history must be seen. From the Gospel and from a common faith they offer the criterion for understanding the Gospel in common faith.

The Christological statements of the Apostles' Creed are not intended to say all that can be said about Jesus Christ. They do not preach all that the tradition preached. And above all, their purpose is not to document historic events in which one must "believe." Their meaning and their aim is to formulate the essential presupposition and foundation of the person and history of Jesus Christ according to the church's preaching of the faith as this is supported in the Gospel and to formulate it in confessional statements—that is, in binding statements of affirmation and praise. In this way they point to the truth of the unspoken history of Jesus Christ and allow him to appear now and forever in the reality of what he is. It is precisely in connection with this essential definition of Jesus Christ that the Christological creed very early—from the beginning in fact—included statements about God the Father, the almighty Creator of heaven and earth, and later about the Holy Spirit.

If we accept this, then we need not be surprised that the Apostles' Creed (and the earlier creeds) proceed directly from Christ's birth to his death and resurrection. We find that we must read all of the Christological formulas of the creeds in close connection with the apostolic preaching out of which they arose in the form of essential definitions. So we must read our particular article on the death of Jesus in the light of what is unsaid, in connection with what this death ends and fulfills; in connection, therefore, with the works and the way of Jesus.

In other words, we have to understand the words "who suffered under Pontius Pilate, was crucified, dead, and buried" as the result of Jesus' way and works, as the effective purpose that lights up the earthly life of Jesus and illuminates the event that is Jesus Christ. It is necessary to read the Gospel of Jesus' death as an all-embracing interpretation. The Apostles' Creed never loses sight of the way that Jesus went to the cross with mighty word and sign and in obedience to God. But the Creed does not speak of this, only of its end as that in which everything else is determined and revealed as a unity. It explains the essence of the way and works of Jesus.

But let us examine the article itself. It obviously values the fact that Jesus' death, which it confesses, is an event on earth which can be historically dated: "under Pontius Pilate." Why is Pontius Pilate in the Creed? He simply serves as a date, nothing more than this. His name establishes that the death of Jesus is a fact of concrete history. "Suffered under Pontius Pilate" means the years between 26 and 36/37 when he was Roman procurator in Judea. But the naming of his name probably has another significance as well. It shows that this dated death was not history in some desolate spot far from the public and official world, but an event in which even the Imperium, the "state," encountered Jesus in its representative who stood before truth personified, as St. John's Gospel puts it, and who was ruined by this truth.

This statement of the Creed also emphasizes the reality of

Jesus' dying. We can still trace the expansion of this description within the evolution of the Creed, while the individual ideas were threatened with the loss of their specific meaning and their expressive power as summary of a whole process. Originally—that is, in the pre-New Testament formulas of faith—the ideas "suffered," "crucified," and "died" described the total event of Christ's death, each from a different tradition. So the idea "suffering" referred to the death as a whole, for example, for the evangelist Luke and in the formulation used by 1 Peter. "Cross" and "crucify" are primarily the Pauline symbol for this same death. "Die" is obviously a general description of the event of Jesus' death, principally in connection with resurrection from the dead. For the rest, burial is mentioned in the most ancient creedal formulas. But now in the Apostles' Creed, and even to some extent in its various pre-formulations, these summarizing ideas were all listed together, so that they lost some of their comprehensive and yet specific significance. Indeed, thereby the event of Jesus' death is given its full weight, and its reality becomes more vivid by way of this expansion as far as the laconic style of the Creed will allow. Here "suffered" no longer refers to the death of Jesus as such, but to his passion as reported by the Gospels. The death is included in the suffering unto death; denial by the disciples, false accusations, false judgment, ridicule, and derision, blows, wounds, thirst, and finally abandonment even by God. "Died" refers to the end of suffering, the end of life: he inclined his head and died. And that this is an irrevocable and definitive end on earth is clearly expressed in the word "buried." Now there is no hope for Jesus in the world. His last place on earth is the grave.

Between "suffered" and "died" we still find "crucified." Isn't that really superfluous? In the course of events, the cross was simply a link joining suffering and death. In the so-called "Romanum" (creed), we find only *crucifixus et sepultus,* and this covers everything. Why bother keeping *crucifixus* in the Apostles' Creed, since "suffered" takes its place? Why? Because faith recognizes in the Cross of Jesus the key to his death; in other words, because for faith the Cross is a sign which points to the meaning of the event as a whole. The Cross reveals the death of Jesus as a consequence of human guilt. Man looked upon him in whom they encountered the justice of God and his faithfulness in truth and love as a criminal and hung him up to die. But the Cross also reveals the death of Jesus as a consequence of divine love. God's love sustains men in all that they do, and all that they do is taken to death and the grave in the body of Jesus Christ; all the evil of their hearts and looks, of their tongues and hands, is buried with him. In an ancient confessional hymn handed down to us in the First Letter of Peter, it says, "He carried the burden of our sins in his own body on the Cross, in order that we might die to sin and live for justice. By his wounds you have been healed." The Cross places the question about Jesus' death vividly and inescapably; the question is whether we will accept the death and thereby accept our guilt and the surpassing love of God. The Cross remains the everpresent critical question asked of man. Will he, as St. Paul says of the Jews and the pagans, stumble on it or ridicule it, or will he, as the Christian, confess it in the single words of the Apostles' Creed: "Suffered under Pontius Pilate, Was crucified, dead, and buried." Then perhaps he will hear also how it goes on: "The third day He arose again from the dead."

JÜRGEN MOLTMANN

He descended into hell...

If we enter a church and hear a sermon on hell, many of us laugh and shrug our shoulders: "Where can it be, this 'hell,' where the evil devil tortures the miserable souls and roasts them in fire? That is a fairy tale to frighten children with. But we are adult, enlightened, and mature. Nothing can scare us." The hell threatened by the church does not exist. When we enter a church today, therefore, we can be pretty certain that there will be no talk of hell.

But is there nothing like hell any more? After the other world has become dark we have managed to make this world and this life into a hell, have paved it with hells. We talk of the "hell of Auschwitz," and we know that the most diabolical imagination is incapable of picturing the unjustifiable, senseless mass death, the planned and horrible mass murder. We walk over the fields of death of the world wars. There was the "hell of Verdun," then the "hell of Stalingrad," now the "green hell of Vietnam." We hear the gasp of the dying, the scream of the tortured. Injustice cries to heaven. Suffering has no answer. Even we find no meaning here, for there is none. "Abandon all hope, you who enter here" was written above Dante's hell, and we know that the history in which we find ourselves carries this same motto. This is why we become so often apathetic. "Remember the darkness and the bitter cold," said Brecht. We do not like to remember it, but we know that it is there surrounding us on all sides. "Condemned for all eternity," now that we do not hear this in church any more, it is shouted to us in films, plays, and books.

But we do not have to go so far, we do not have to depend on experiencing at second hand a certain measure of alienation.

"Hell is other people," proclaims Sartre in a play produced after the war. How often do we complain to one another, "You make my life a hell." Whenever men live close together they can prepare for themselves a heaven on earth, but they can also turn life into a hell. Man expects recognition and friendliness, and suddenly there is only complete contempt and uncontrollable fury. A lostness rises to the surface, a lostness that struggles and fights out of pure anxiety. This is the experience of hell. It is not simply a legend. Gently but inexorably it undermines man's happiness and turns the warm hunger for life into a pitiful hatred of life. And there is something else: We are not only its victims, we also stoke its fires. No one can guarantee us that the "hell of Auschwitz" will not return. No one can be sure that he will never more turn the life of his neighbour into a hell.

So we see that what we thought was far away is very close, and what we thought was a fairy tale is reality. Martin Luther expressed it in classic form in one of his hymns:

> In the midst of life we are surrounded by death.
> In the midst of death we are under hell's vengeance.
> In the midst of hell we are ridden by anxiety for our sins.

Death is in the midst of life. Hell is the torment of this death in the midst of life: to live and not to be able to live, to love and not to be able to love, to help and not to be able to help: this becomes the anguish that has no name. Its thorn is guilt, the fiery torture of a bungled life. That is why all hells depend on us. "I do not do the good things that I want to do; I do the wrong things that I do not want to do" (Romans 8:19).

Luther's hymn converts this realistic insight into a cry to infinity: "Whom do we seek who will help us to obtain grace? Who will free us from our need? Where can we go to be safe?" Is there any answer? Would life still be a hell if we knew the answer? And if we ourselves answer by promising, no more war, never again Auschwitz, no more making life hell for others—are we then safe from hell's evil, which threatens to submerge us? Are we sure of ourselves? In the face of our contemporary experience of hell the usual religious answers and the usual moralistic answers are pale and empty.

But if these answers no longer satisfy, then the question still remains: To whom do we go? Where can we find him? Who will free us from our need?

What do Christians mean when they believe that Jesus, whom they call the Son of God, "descended into hell"? Is this the answer? Is it a valid answer? Let us check a few facts to find out what is really meant here.

The Synod of Sirmium in 359 first added this article to the Creed. The Syrian theologian Markus of Arethusa proposed it. He intended it to mean that Jesus, the Son of God, really died. In his suffering, crucifixion, and burial he actually experienced in himself the absolute pain of abandonment by God. Christ's descent into hell indicates the depth of his suffering. It does not mean a journey through the mythical kingdom of the separated souls. "Suffered—crucified—died": what really occurred there was Christ's entry into the hell of guilt, of pain, of death and beyond. Christ is not so divine that all of this had no effect upon him. He is divine precisely inasmuch as, despite all these hells, he became our brother. This was the original significance of the faith in Christ's descent into hell.

The Latin church of the West, however, very soon interpreted it in another way. There the descent into hell came to mean the triumphal journey of the Redeemer through the land of the dead, the victorious conquest of hell, the liberation of the captives from the old alliance, especially of Adam and Eve. The descent into hell became the first stage of his ascension in which he became Lord of all, of the living and the dead. Nothing is beyond the pale of his redeeming might. Death and hell are no limits to his power, which reached out to all. So in the First Epistle to Peter we read that Christ preached to the imprisoned spirits who had been disobedient. And "the good news was preached to the dead also" and salvation came to them. Christ had mastered death in his own body, so that he had the "key to hell and to death" in his hand. The dead, the murdered, the gassed are not lost. Whether all will be saved we do not know.

Both ideas, that of Christ's descent into hell as the epitome of his suffering on the Cross of abandonment by God and that of Christ's ascension as the beginning of his resurrection for the salvation of all, run through the history of the Christian faith. Luther and Calvin understood them in the light of the cross, as did Markus of Arethusa. The Lutheran theology of the seventeenth century understood them in the light of the resurrection. But whether the accent was on the suffering of hell's torments on the cross or on the triumph of Christ over hell, both ideas had some truth in them.

This is understandable when we examine the reality of Jesus' dying next to the criminals before the gate of Jerusalem. Jesus died the death of one banished. Condemned by his own people in the name of God's law, he died as one cursed and abandoned by God. He was given over to the Romans and disgraced by them with crucifixion. What is special about this death? On the Appian Way, seven thousand were crucified after the uprising of Spartacus. The peculiarity of Jesus' death lies in the one who was dishonoured and abandoned. Jesus was the one who proclaimed the nearness of God's kingdom and who had lived wholly in this nearness. God is with man. That is why Jesus forgave sin as God did, was gracious to the poor and to prostitutes and publicans as God was, and interpreted the law in freedom as God did. When he died as a criminal, his death was marked by something common to no other death—namely, the experience of being abandoned by that same God whose nearness he had proclaimed. This was the experience of abandonment in the clear consciousness that God was not far but wholly near. And this very fact of being excluded from God's presence in the full consciousness of God's closeness *is* the torment of hell. No one can be more abandoned than he who was so at home with God. This is why Christians have always taken courage from the fact that Jesus was the most tormented and the most abandoned of all those who have God and life and who yet find hell and death. Albert Camus also understood it in this way in his sympathy not for God but for the crucified, sympathy in the fellowship of the tormented.

Another approach is the triumphal understanding of Christ's descent into hell. For in this case faith stresses the fact that God brought back from the dead and from hell this most abandoned of all men. Since God proved his nearness and his liberating power in regard to this man, then the hell experienced by him in solidarity with all condemned men is no longer what it used to be. Then because of this miserable one a kingdom has appeared for all in the midst of hell, a kingdom of peace and joy and laughter. Hell is broken and mastered in him. No longer is it horror without end, for he is the beginning of the end of all horrors. The sufferings of hell are no longer eternal nor are they the final word. "Death has been triumphantly destroyed. Where, death, is your sting?" are the words Paul uses in his First Epistle to the Corinthians to taunt death. Hell is open. Man is free to pass through it. And this is true not only of his hell but of all hells on earth. Since God has foreshadowed his future through the crucified one, the glimmer of dawn has begun to break above the fields of death and the places of murder, and also above the little hells of everyday life.

If we compare the faith in the Christ who descended into hell with the hell that makes our life on earth unbearable, then we find the courage to identify the Crucified with those who suffer. Christ was not crucified between two candles on the altar but between two exiles on a rocky hill outside the city. He has become the brother of the abandoned, the lonely, the tortured, the innocent who are murdered and the guilty who are despised. He is on their side, not on the other. They may be in the fear of hell, but they are not alone. God has left his high place and is present with his abandoned ones. Our God is there, in the disgraced, in the beaten, in those whose life we have turned into hell. This means that we should not look to ourselves, fixed in the moment of our misery on earth. "Look to the wounds of Christ, for there has your hell been mastered" (Luther). God enters hell, and hell is consumed in him; this is what Christ's descent into hell means. Not that we or others are spared torment, but with our faith we can pass through in freedom. "He goes through death, through world, sin and need, he goes through hell; I am always with him" (Paul Gerhardt).

There is one more thing that we must say: If Christ is truly risen from death and hell, this means that our conscience should rise against the hells on earth and against all who fire them. For the rising of this condemned man is witnessed to and accomplished by rising against man's condemnation of man. The more firmly our hope believes in the powerlessness of hell, the more militant it should be in destroying all hells—the white, the black, the green, the noisy, and the silent. The Christ who descended into hell is not only consolation in suffering; he is the passionate protest of God against immersion in suffering.

GÜNTHER BORNKAMM

The third day He rose again from the dead...

In primitive Christianity the confession of Christ's resurrection from the dead was not just one article of faith among many others but the basic content of the whole faith and of all confessions. So Paul could write in his Epistle to the Romans: "For if with your lips you acknowledge the message that Jesus is Lord, and with your mind you believe that God raised him from the dead, you will be saved" (Romans 10:9). And the same apostle, with unmistakable clarity and sharpness, declared in 1 Corinthians 15: "If Christ was not raised, there is nothing in our message; there is nothing in our faith either...." For, he goes on, then we apostles have fallen prey to error and deception and have lied to you. We have become God's enemies, for he has nothing to do with our message. Then we Christians are the most miserable of all men and should free ourselves of his web of illusions and return to the at least honest word of the unbeliever: "Let us eat and drink, for tomorrow we die." It is not the apostle's intention to offer a positive proof of the truth of the Christian message by way of the unbearableness of its denial, somewhat in the spirit of the widespread but questionable argumentation: What way is left to us, if all this is only a lie? On the contrary, instead of the dark possibilities implied in this last question, he emphasizes the clear and unambiguous truth as witnessed to by the whole of early Christianity: "Christ *is* risen." And he declares that it is not our faith in the risen one that is illusion and fantasy but that, on the contrary, we would be victims of illusion and fantasy if we did not believe in and proclaim his resurrection.

It's no secret that for us today the certainty of early Christianity in this matter is astonishing and odd; it makes our approach to the mystery more difficult rather than easier. No one can deny the fact of that certainty, nor can anyone deny that without it there would be no such thing as Christianity —up to this very day. We could not concern ourselves with this ancient confession of the faith unless that astonishing message had been the object of proclamation and belief since the first days. But an earlier generation's certainty in faith is not necessarily a certainty for us too. How can we approach this mystery? We must return to the texts of the New Testament.

Whoever reads these two texts not only for edification but with the historical-critical attitude demanded by the New Testament taken as historical testimony can easily see that various texts differ greatly in style and time of composition. It is generally recognized that the oldest and historically the most reliable testimony is a formula of faith of which Paul reminds the congregation in 1 Corinthians 15: " . . . that Christ died for our sins, as the scriptures foretold, that he was buried, that on the third day he was raised from the dead, as the scriptures foretold, and that he was seen by Cephas (that is Peter). . . ." Then follows a whole chain of eyewitnesses and a whole list of appearances up to the final appearance of the Lord to Paul himself.

Many things are important about this text. I will mention but a few of its significant characteristics, and, first of all, its antiquity. Paul assures us that he received this formula of faith and passed it on, so that it surely goes back to the earliest postpaschal period of the primitive community. Next we note the large number of witnesses to the appearances of the resurrected Christ. Then, its fundamental place in the faith of every Christian. Finally, regarding its content, it is noteworthy that this formula speaks only of the appearance of Christ, but not, for example, of the discovery of the empty grave by the women on Easter morning, as we read in the Gospels. It is most likely that Paul knew nothing of this account, which is one of a series of Easter stories that were first written down decades after the Pauline text.

In comparison with the fairly uniform tradition of the history of the passion, the tradition of these stories is rather manifold. From one Gospel to the other and finally to the later apocryphal tradition of the ancient church, one can clearly observe the growth of paschal stories with the most diverse tendencies and not without the influence of colourful legends. These are not only quite different from the Pauline text, but they show considerable variation even among themselves.

Does this tradition allow us to say anything historically reliable about the course of the resurrection event? Not with certainty, in any case. Remarkably enough, the New Testament accounts say absolutely nothing about the actual course of the event. The later and less refined tradition put this hesitation aside, and even in the New Testament we find some legendary characteristics. According to the church historian Hans von Campenhausen, the most ancient form of the story of the empty grave, in St. Mark's Gospel, was intended to establish the historicity of the unexplainable fact that the grave of Jesus had to be empty on Easter morning and that this was the motive for the journey of the disciples to Jerusalem, where most of the appearances of the resurrected one took place. It is true that none of the texts that describe or mention those appearances ever refer to the story of the grave. And equally possible—and in my opinion more probable—is the opinion of many scholars that the story of the empty grave and the explanation given by the angel represents an attempt to make the miracle of Jesus' resurrection more credible and convincing and to defend it against false interpretation by the Jews.

What do we learn from an examination of the historical tradition? First of all, we see that by reason of its antiquity the unanimous and unambiguous Easter message of primitive Christianity as represented in the text of Paul takes preference over the later and widely diverging reports. This does not mean that the Easter stories in the Gospels lose their value or significance. It simply means that, from the viewpoint of history, we are not on solid ground here.

But what does this mean for the faith? Doesn't it take the ground out from under the faith? This is the viewpoint of that unbelief which uses the results of exegetical research to its own advantage. This is also the viewpoint of a certain widespread variety of Christian belief, though it draws the opposite conclusion; historical-critical biblical research is a dangerous and destructive business, and faith should hold its front by maintaining as certain and secure what is historically unsure. But is this the faith demanded of us by the New Testament? Certainly not! Then faith would be no more than an act of violence against the historical reason and would be forced to preserve itself by maintaining a past occurrence which the historian holds as doubtful or at least improbable (here, the empty grave) for an absolutely certain fact. As if faith stands or falls on the basis of whether a particular event in the past happened precisely in this way or that!

One often misses the fact that in this unanimity of disbelief and alleged faith both sides are looking to the empty grave and both fall subject to the judgment of the angel's words, "Why seek the living among the dead?" No, the truth of the Easter message has to be decided elsewhere. Historical-critical research in itself can offer no proof of it. The truth of the message of Easter is accessible only to faith. But what is the truth and reality of this message? The texts of the New Testament say that it lies in the fact that the disciples, strangely enough, after the definitive catastrophe—in human eyes—of Golgotha, encountered their Lord anew. In this encounter they became aware that God had acknowledged him whom the world had refused to acknowledge, and that Christ was not the conquered but the conqueror, not destroyed by death, but the living one, present among them with his Word and the power of his Spirit. To speak here of simple visions or projections of their own credulousness goes beyond the bounds of historical knowledge as much as every attempt to establish the historical course of the Resurrection in the same manner as an ordinary occurrence. Faith is not interested in the tricks of psychological explanations. And even the historian would do well to speak of an event here, however difficult it may be for him to describe it in the usual categories. In the final analysis, however, faith can speak about the resurrection of Jesus and its revelation before the disciples only as a miraculous act of God, just as the Creed says: "The third day He arose again from the dead." For this much is certain and is confirmed by all the Easter texts, that the disciples in their miraculous encounter with their resurrected Lord brought with them nothing but anxiety and despair, and it was not, as Faust says, that "They celebrated the resurrection of the Lord because they themselves had risen." After the horrors of Jesus' passion and death, their faith had not sustained them nor enabled them to recover from the shock and later to interpret the end of their Lord as being conciliating after all. On the contrary, their faith was revived by the living Lord, and they recognized that it was they who had fallen in death while the resurrected one was Lord of death and of the world. And there was more than just this astounding contrast. There was also the fact that he called *them* to life. "I live on, and you shall live on too!" (John 14:19).

Resurrection from the dead is completely different from the Greek idea of the immortality of the soul. For the Greeks death did not disturb the soul, but liberated it from the prison of the mortal body. But when the Bible talks of resurrection it refers to the miracle of the new creation of the whole man through death to a new life by the power of God. However much the expressions current in those days influenced the Bible, what was decisive was not the expression but that which they were intended to express: the redeeming and liberating penetration of our world and history by the world of God. Not only a rare occurrence long ago, and not at all the miracle of a temporary return of a dead man among the living, the resurrection of Jesus meant nothing less than the end of world and history.

This statement may seem utterly fantastic and it may appear that the advance of history through the centuries contradicts it. By "the end of the world and its history," though, the New Testament does not at all mean that the clock of history is stopped or that henceforth there can no longer be any yesterday, today, and tomorrow. If this were what it really meant, then the Christian faith would have collapsed long ago. The end of world and history means that the alienating and enslaving powers which in the eyes of men had imprisoned the world and human existence, which had seduced, enchanted, terrified, and threatened man and world with death, were conquered and the way was opened to the freedom of God's creatures and children. This can be understood only in faith, often against all appearances and even against the experience of one's own heart. And yet faith holds on to it and does not give it up and knows that the world can never lose this promise of God and its sign of hope. Since Easter, the faithful stand before the appeal, the promise, and the question of Jesus Christ: whether they will let his life and his lordship affect their own existence and whether they will look upon the world as the field of their Lord's victory.

We know now that faith in the resurrection of Christ can never mean the maintenance and defence of a tissue of ancient and miraculous events, but the preservation of the liberating Word for the sake of the world and the confiding of oneself to this Word. This is why the New Testament says of the faithful: "He has caused us to be born anew to a life of hope, protected through faith in the power of God" (1 Peter 1:3ff.).

ANTON VÖGTLE

He ascended into heaven . . .

Few phrases of the Apostles' Creed are more perfect examples of the attachment of the Christian message to a long obsolete image of the world than the phrase "ascended into heaven."

How can we take this statement seriously today? In this century of space travel, we all know that the earth is a sphere, not a disk above which there stretches the massive shell of the firmament with God's throne room. What does it mean, then, when the Acts of the Apostles tells us: "And as he said this, he was caught up before their eyes and a cloud took him up from their sight. And while they were gazing after him into the sky, two men dressed in white suddenly stood beside them and said: 'Men of Galilee, why do you stand looking up into the sky? This very Jesus who has been caught up from you into heaven will come in just the way that you have seen him go up to heaven' " (1:9–11).

Without any doubt, this is an occurrence that can only be described as a miracle, and a double miracle at that. Before the eyes of his disciples, Jesus floated upwards—however briefly this is mentioned and however much the cloud hid the actual event. But this is not all! As a *deus ex machina,* two angels appeared suddenly beside the astonished disciples—for the two men in white are obviously angels according to customary biblical expression. Obviously this event was visible and audible. There is unusual emphasis on the vision of the disciples: "before their eyes"—"from their sight"—"gazing up"—"looking up." And the phrase: "And while they were gazing after him into the sky" obviously calls to mind the image of a prolonged flight upwards. But this could not be a literal report of the occurrence, you say. In reality, it is merely a figurative expression for an event which essentially defies description. But if phrases such as "he was caught up" and "before their eyes" mean what they usually do, then the author must have been reporting about an empirically observed event. So the only alternative is: Did it happen or not; is it merely a deceit, a flight of imagination, a legend or myth?

Oh, I cannot really blame the stranger to theology for this way of thinking. It is only right that he should reason this way, as long as he is unfamiliar with the various functions of the story form in the ancient and especially in the biblical world. For in these worlds not everything that is presented as a visible and invisible occurrence actually refers to an empirically observable event in the world of phenomena. And this is particularly true of the occurrence of the resurrection and the appearances of the resurrected one, which the New Testament clearly characterizes as the effects of a wholly miraculous act of God. It is inevitable that the layman will get the wrong impression unless he comes to realize how the whole New Testament speaks of Jesus' resurrection, and the special intention that particularly motivates Luke, who is the only New Testament author who offers an extended account of the ascension (which he describes with considerable artistic talent), and unless he becomes aware of the current themes and means of expression at the author's disposal and which of these he actually used in order to speak of the resurrection out of his own situation. The key to the whole problem is to find out how the author himself understood what he said!

But before we examine Luke more closely we will first look at the other New Testament writers (though excluding Mark 16:19 which assumed the Lukan ascension theme). None of them mentions a forty-day period of Easter appearances concluded by an ascension. Not that the idea of Jesus' "ascension" was foreign to them! For Paul, just as for Matthew and John, and for the entire New Testament *kerygma*, Jesus, from the very moment of his resurrection, ascended into heaven. The "resurrection" is identified with his elevation to the heavens, his enthronement, his establishment in power as the Son of God—just to mention the most important images used in the *kerygma* to express one and the same event. And this resurrection—this establishment in power—is understood wholly as an otherworldly process, of whose truth those who witnessed to the appearances have been convinced by the self-revelation of the resurrected one, but which in itself was no more an object of empirical observation than God himself or "the right hand" of God. When the resurrected one appears, he appears always from heaven, as the elevated one, so that it is unnecessary to say of the appearances before the disciples and before Paul that as a finale to the appearances Jesus returned to heaven or that he was "caught up," but only that, as in both of Luke's writings, he "vanished from them" (Luke 24:31).

Why then does Luke and only he let the resurrected one go up to heaven at the end of his last appearances? Because Luke, in accord with the aim of his two writings and especially that of the Acts of the Apostles, wants to stress in a vivid way definite aspects of the significance of Jesus' resurrection and elevation. Only he mentions the forty days during which Jesus manifested himself as living to his apostles and spoke to them of the Kingdom of God (Acts 1:5). This unique mention of forty days was not for Luke an exact measurement of time but, according to common usage in Scripture, an approximate and sacred designation for a long interval. By way of this holy number Luke wanted to underline the decisive salvational-historical temper of the time of the appearances. For this was the time during which the disciples became convinced of the reality of Jesus' resurrection and during which they received the commission to propagate, in the power the Holy Spirit, the message of God's kingdom in accord with the salvific situation as confirmed by Good Friday and Easter. That the appearances of the resurrected one formed the basis for the "apostolate," the mission, the conferring of the power, and the obligation to proselytize is the common conviction of the New Testament writers, Paul no less than the Evangelists. The important thing about the departure speech in Acts 1:4–8 is the response given by the Christ-revelation itself to the initial hope for a swift return of Christ: First must come a time of unknown duration, a time of mission in the power of the Spirit, the time of the church, during which Jesus stays in heaven and leaves his "chosen apostles" their present task.

This is why Luke combines the departure scene and the ascension, whose observable elements he uses to serve his interpretation. When he says that a cloud obscures the risen one who is being carried up, Luke is not thinking of a metereological phenomenon that stood in the heavens or was magically produced by God in the right place at the right time. With the common biblical motif, he means to say that "the real event of the ascension, Christ's assumption into the glory of God and into the inner circle of his might, is an impenetrable mystery for man" (Gerhard Lohfink). Together with this intention, it is also possible that Luke uses the symbol of a cloud to point to the return in power of the resurrected one. In his emphasis on vision, therefore, it was not his purpose to claim that the event was empirically observable. He wanted much more to underline the witness of the disciples and, beyond this, to prepare the way for his interpretation of the ascension as spoken through the angels, the usual biblical interpreters of wholly mysterious occurrences. The elevation of Jesus into heaven guarantees his return in divine power and glory. "This very Jesus who has been caught up from you into heaven will come in just the way that you have seen him go up to heaven." The rejection of the human question regarding the time of the final revelation (Acts 1:6–8), the dampening of the intense expectation of the *parousia,* does not at all mean—and this is what Luke intends to stress—the rejection of belief in the Lord's return, which is an incontestable truth of Christian faith. The thought of the Lord's return can only increase the readiness of the faithful to attend to the problems of the moment. The order of the day becomes: "Back to work! Why do you stand looking up into the sky?" Now that the Easter appearances are over, it is time to bear witness in the power of the Spirit to the resurrection of the crucified Jesus "in Jerusalem, in all of Judea and Samaria, and to the ends of the earth," as Luke had expressed the course of the Christian mission, thereby formulating the programme of his double tract of missionary recruitment (Acts 1:8).

Luke's description of the ascension, therefore, does refer to a real and wholly miraculous event: Jesus' elevation to a heavenly mode of existence. But it is not a report of a visible and audible occurrence; with the help of the above-mentioned images—the gazing disciples, the cloud, the interpreting angels—Luke intended to interpret the resurrection of Christ theologically and above all to show its significance for the further course of history after Easter.

Yes, you may object, this is what modern exegetes who want to make the faith acceptable and who have an astounding talent for sidestepping the most unmanageable difficulties say. But if you are sceptical of this interpretation, then let Luke speak for himself. For however much he tries, in vivid and imaginative descriptions of the appearances, to underline their reality, and to negate the objection of self-deception on the part of the disciples, it does not even enter his mind to patch up the guilt of the Christian Easter *kerygma* with the affirmation that Jesus went up to heaven and took on a heavenly mode of existence only forty days after Easter as a conclusion to his Easter appearances. Luke, as the other authors of the New Testament, knew nothing of an interim condition in which Jesus remained between his resurrection and his elevation to heaven. Luke's Gospel and Acts show very clearly that Jesus' resurrection already signified his elevation and enthronement at the right hand of God and that, for Luke, the resurrected one appeared always as from heaven: "Did not the Christ have to suffer thus before entering upon his glory?" the resurrected one says in Luke 24:26 during his first appearance.

In conclusion, one more question: shouldn't we reformulate this article of the Apostles' Creed in view of the fact that "ascended into heaven" does not really refer to an external event in earthly space but, with the help of the then current image of a three-layered universe, to a purely otherworldly happening? I cannot think of an adequate substitute, nor do I feel that it is really needed. Whether we use ancient or contemporary images has little to do with the reality involved! And an event that is beyond all conceivable earthly dimensions defies adequate description in any case. How can we speak of this event in any way which differs essentially from that of the New Testament authors? We can better use the imaginative expression, largely inspired by Old Testament prophecy: elevated by God, placed at God's right hand, established as God's Son, ascended into heaven.

HANS CONZELMANN

And sitteth on the right hand of God the Father Almighty; From thence He shall come to judge the quick and the dead

If we assume the hypothesis that the Apostles' Creed is an adequate summary of Christian faith, then this article on the "last judgment" is the least satisfying doctrine of this faith. It seems to question the very *raison d'être* of faith itself. It does not say: "to judge the godless," but *all,* whether Christian or non-Christian, evangelical, Catholic, Marxist, Muslim, saints or criminals, monks or worldlings. So what good is faith if I have to go on trial just like everyone else and do not know what the judgment on me is going to be? This article seems to threaten the very core of religion. After all, we do not expect that religion can give us security in the future, even beyond death. Yet here I am faced with a trial and thrown into uncertainty. Isn't this simply an inhuman game with human anxiety? As if we didn't have enough on our shoulders already, whether we like to admit it or prefer not to face it.

The innumerable medieval (and later) paintings of judgment, heaven, and hell, illustrate for us the enormous burden of anxiety which weighted the minds and hearts of men for centuries. And when contemporary philosophy turns against Christianity, it is with a conviction that promises freedom from anxiety. Man himself is the only authority to whom he must answer, in the free maintenance of his personal integrity and not as the helpless victim of a verdict pronounced by a stranger who is above all appeal.

Even in Christian thought the notion of the judgment is falling more and more into disuse. It plays hardly any role in the public discussion on the nature of Christianity. The average Christian finds it a painful subject, so he does not talk about it. The only time it is ever taken out of the Christian storehouse is in case of need; every once in a while churchmen find it necessary that the "church" direct a penitential word to the "world." But in our "normal" attitude, there is no longer any place for it. If we let our minds go, free from the prescription of ecclesiastical teaching, and think our own thoughts about God and man, then the idea of a judgment of the world seems foreign to our time, inadequate to man, and unbecoming to God. God, if he exists at all, should be a good father who lives above the firmament and who takes care to compensate man for the disillusionments of life. God has to pay back and not claim debts!

Over the last two centuries Christianity has undergone a process of intellectual contraction. In public opinion the Christian message has been largely narrowed down to three points:

First of all, there is a God, a higher being. This is not an exclusive or original Christian idea, and it is doubtful whether it is worth offering one's head for it.

Secondly, man possesses an immortal soul. We may consider this to be a beautiful, uplifting, and profound thought, in any case, it is surely not Christian. There is not even a hint of it in the Bible or in the Creed; in fact it is excluded by faith in the resurrection of the dead. The Christian profession of faith says that man is wholly subject to death because he has fallen into sin, and that he gains eternal salvation when he wins forgiveness of guilt by being declared innocent in the judgment of God.

Thirdly, another element of average religiosity is the spiritual freedom and moral responsibility of man. This is no peculiarly Christian notion either. As true as it is that I am responsible for my actions, it is just as clear that Christianity teaches that man has lost his freedom. But as we have said, these uncomfortable aspects of faith are coated in the average Christian consciousness with the conviction that God is a "loving God" and that everything will come out all right after death—provided that one has taken the trouble to end one's life as a decent person.

Is this really an improvement on the earlier, outmoded attitude toward the last judgment? In any case, it is not a simple matter. Here and there we notice symptoms of a remarkable schizophrenia which extends far beyond the circle of those who call themselves Christians; even those who consider themselves spiritually emancipated and up-to-date expect the church and her pastors to think conservatively, in mythical expression. Why? Obviously to secure for themselves a last refuge, in case—in case it might be true after all, in case one really does have to encounter God after death. So let us try to find out what truth there is in the notion that God is a judge to whom we will have to answer.

First of all, there is no *scientific* proof for such a statement, just as there is none for the existence of God or for any truth of the Christian faith. How then can it be proved?

This question can be answered only if the God-man relationship as a whole is considered. In the profession of faith it is not a question of doctrines on the construction of the universe, blueprints of heaven and hell, or prognoses of the future development of nature and history. It is rather a question of the disclosure of what God means for our existence now and in the future, a question of faith, hope, and love, a question of the present as our God-given chance to make something of our humanity and of the future that reaches beyond the limits of our experience and beyond death. We do not understand the articles of the Creed if we insist on forming images of heaven and hell and God and the devil. They are purely imaginative. We do understand them, however, if we recognize in our own existence what is true and false and what is salvation and damnation, when we recognize them as landmarks along the way from birth to death. We find ourselves in "heaven" when we experience that God is with us, the God of the Creed, the Creator and Father who declared through Christ what he intended for us. It is characteristic of the Creed that it does not say we shall be judged by God, but by Jesus Christ. This does not mean that God is excluded. It means that the relation between God and ourselves is governed, even in the future, by the same principles that were laid down in Christ, the human God who was murdered. This article on the judgment can be understood only in the light of the preceding articles, and all of them can be summarized in the crowning affirmation that Jesus Christ is Lord.

This means that God is not the ancient figure with flowing beard who lives in majestic separation from the world. His voice is heard in the world, and through Christ we know what he says. The measure of life allotted to us, the measure of effort demanded of us, and the measure of fulfilment granted to us is not the measure of the world—the measure of power and success—but the measure of the man Jesus Christ who failed and was destroyed, who annulled the history of debt and established free entry to God.

"Sitteth on the right hand of God" is the bridge from past (died, rose, ascended) to present; on the right hand is the place of honour. From Jesus, God's representative to the world, we learn what is in store for us.

The bow is bent still further, over the present and into the future: "from thence he shall come. . . ." This means that if we believe in Christ's resurrection and lordship, then we believe in our own resurrection. And if we look to the judgment, we hope in eternal salvation. But is this not a contradiction? Is not the forgiveness of guilt and the sureness of hope contradicted by the judgment? Or are we left in an unbearable tension between fear and hope, an inhuman situation that calls our feelings to revolt?

The apparent contradiction is resolved in the oneness of him who both forgives and judges. We cannot understand this if we begin with imagining a judgment and a judge; rather we have to begin by realizing that the person of Christ defines what judgment is in the first place. Judgment does not revoke the given forgiveness of guilt; it is the final phase of guilt's removal. This means that I have access to God, that I have been granted the freedom to lay bare the roots of my life and to stand before God as I really am, the guilty one who has won the chance through faith to freely confess my guilt. The judgment is the opportunity in the future to stand before God in freedom and without illusion and to confess my guilt. In this sense, the expectation of the judgment is transformed into freedom in the world: freedom from the illusion of hiding my guilt from myself, freedom to stand for the truth in a hopeless situation, freedom to serve my fellow man without profit and even with danger to myself. The expectation of the judgment makes me free for death. In Paul's Epistle to the Romans (8:31-39) we find the unsurpassable explanation of the interplay of salvation and judgment:

> "If God is for us, who can be against us? Did not he who did not spare his own Son, but gave him up for us all, with that gift give us *everything*? Who can bring any accusation against those whom God has chosen? *God* pronounces them upright; who can condemn them? Christ Jesus who died, or rather who was raised from the dead, is at God's right hand, and actually *pleads for us*. Who can separate us from Christ's love? Can trouble or misfortune or persecution or hunger or destitution or danger of the sword? As the Scripture says, 'For your sake we are being put to death all day long, we are treated like sheep to be slaughtered!' But in all these things we are more than victorious through him who loved us. For I am convinced that neither death nor life nor angels nor their hierarchies nor the present nor the future nor any supernatural force either of height or depth nor anything else in creation will be able to separate us from the love God has shown us in Christ Jesus our Lord!"

This passage should suffice to explain our article of the Creed, but the art of reading the Bible has become uncommon; even in the church there is little demand for it any more.

WALTER DIRKS

I believe in the Holy Ghost . . .

The Christian usually regards faith in the Holy Spirit as being of a different level than that of the first Christological part of theology. He hears of it in the catechism when mother speaks for the first time about the "third person" in the one divinity. She refers to him later and in a different way than to the Father and the Son. More than any other statement of the Apostles' Creed, this one about the Holy Spirit is connected to one of the most delicate of theological issues: the doctrine of the Trinity.

All other articles of the Creed, perhaps with the exception of the one about the descent into hell, are easily assimilated into one's growing understanding of the faith. And this is true also of the testimonies of Scripture. What we read about God's "Spirit" in the Old Testament and even in the New, however, does not easily merge into the one whom we confess as the Holy Spirit. When we hear from the theologians that he is a "person" it becomes disturbingly clear to us how little it means when we transpose an idea developed from man's understanding of himself to the wholly Other. That Jesus is a "person" scarcely troubles the little child; he is after all a man, and even in later life he retains this direct insight. Whoever will find Jesus need only open the Scriptures. Or he can discover him in his fellowmen. With similar ease, the child accepts the "invisible" Father, though this brings problems for the mature Christian: the distinction (without division) between this "first person" and the one God, the tormenting question of the origin and meaning of evil, and the discoveries of depth psychology which have shattered the ancient image of an unproblematical relation between beloved child and loving father.

Still, we follow Jesus when, distinguishing himself from his Father, he speaks about him or teaches us to pray to him or prays to him himself. We follow him and are most impressed by his abandonment in the garden and his preparation for death on the cross. Obviously there are two, a visible and an invisible, who speak to one another; and the Son testifies that these two are one. We do not understand and yet we try to follow. The Son looks like a man and the Father takes the familiar form of a human father.

But nothing can help us to imagine the Holy Spirit. Of the images offered by the Scriptures some are as unintelligible as that of the dove; others are very powerful, such as the storm, the breath, the fire, the light. And yet he remains strange to us, as long as we try to find him outside of ourselves like the Father and the Son.

We live in his era. This is not an unorthodox affirmation of chiliasm and spiritualism; this is the Christian truth. Everything which was placed in motion by Jesus of Nazareth and which has become and is to become reality began with the event of Pentecost. The Spirit will teach us all things; except in him we cannot speak the name of Jesus or that of the Father. The era of the Holy Spirit does not begin in the year 1000 or the year 2000. We live in it now. At the same time, of course, we live in an ambiguous interim kingdom that we think of as between the Ascension and Pentecost. For Pentecost cannot be identified with the life and work of the church and surely not with our own life and work. We "believe" in Jesus and his Father somewhat as the disciples believed in them when Jesus was taken up to the mountain. They were convinced that they believed; they did not deny it and perhaps they did not doubt it, but only at Pentecost did they experience the reality of faith. We do not deny it and usually we do not doubt it, and perhaps we do not doubt even when we are falsely certain of our faith—when we are convinced of an ideological system that we confuse with faith—but only at Pentecost will we experience the reality of faith, perhaps today, perhaps tomorrow. We know and the church knows that this is the time of Pentecost, but it is also the time to say in the expectation of Pentecost: "Lord, I believe, help my unbelief!" and "Come Holy Spirit!" He who is to come is always here. He has been at work and was powerful in the weak, and we can surely say that his work is due equally to the Father. So we see that this first meditation on the Holy Spirit brings us back to the mystery of the trinitarian God.

In discussing the Trinity, theologians have speculated a great deal about the difference between being born and proceeding, about the relations within the Trinity, about intertrinitarian life and most abstractly about the Holy Spirit. But it seems to me that this is above all the place to advocate not trying to master everything with logic and dialectic. Trinitarian theology is often a barrier, a trap, a blind alley, an alibi; the mystery itself, which theology poorly interprets, is what carries and at the same time surpasses our faith. In its non-methodical way Scripture has many different things to say about Father and Son, and the concordance lists a surprisingly large number of entries on the Holy Spirit. It is not only allowed but mandatory to place these various statements in relation, to connect them, to study the apparent contradictions, to combine some in complex intellectual systems and to leave the insoluble elements to be accepted as a mystery. But if one attempts in this way to penetrate intellectually the life of divinity, he not only stumbles at the limits of logic, but he founders on the tempting reef of Gnosticism—or of mockery. I think that it is better for us to try to interpret the word of Scripture from our point of view. God for us—this is not pride; it is a humble and true principle of understanding.

Thereby we inevitably fall into what the orthodox teaching decries as the heresy of modalism: the Father, Son, and Holy Spirit are only modes or manners of appearance, different aspects of the one indivisible God. And yet we surrender this unity—if we are honest about it—in our ordinary behaviour as tri-theists, and even more as bi-theists: simple pious words about the heavenly Father and the beloved Saviour as if they were two Gods. And the Jesus of the Gospels or of the Last Supper and the Creator and Father of all are always two divine archetypes. But if we attempt to hold fast to the truth as revealed to the people of Israel, then our first approach to the trinitarian mystery is in fact modalistic. We distinguish in

God that he is for us: Creator and Father, invisible; the brother beside us, incarnate; the God in us, the Spirit. Only when we remember Jesus' dialogue with his Father are we aware of a correction: the three, whom we distinguished from our point of view, are not divided among themselves. To understand this, the notion of person is of questionable value; if we try to decipher the undecipherable in our human way, the Scriptures and our own religious experience bring us back to a corrected version of modalism as the most human approach to God.

But then the Holy Spirit is the one indivisible God *within us*. He is so close to us that we overlook and forget him. If he is not within us, our faith finds him only with difficulty. All that remains of our relation to him is the pleading cry which he himself has put on our lips: "Come, Holy Spirit!" If he is within us, then he cannot be distinguished from ourselves.

When we live, pray, act, and love in his power, we experience ourselves and not him as the subject of this life. If we try to reflect upon his presence in us, he eludes us; he does not allow himself to be separated from us as something in us. The mystics call him the inner light. It is likely that meditation and its highest form, mystical silence, disclose a little of the mystery of his presence, though we seem to have nearly lost the capacity for letting this happen in our time, and we lack words to describe the beginnings of such an experience. The Holy Spirit is thus the God who appears to be absent by the very fact that he is present. In other words, he is the present God, and he cannot be grasped as an object apart from ourselves. The problem is that I cannot experience God as someone apart from me when he is so close to me.

When Martin Buber and Ernst Michel speak of man as God's partner, and thereby also of their experience of God as man's partner, then they—Buber solely and Michel primarily —refer to God as Father. This is a bold image: we may risk it, but it needs revision. Christ seems close to us in the image of partner because we can think of him as human, as the child in the crib, as the teacher in Galilee and Jerusalem, as dying and even as resurrected. But Christ does not primarily want us to meet him; he wants us to encounter him in our fellowmen, in our brothers and neighbours. We reach Christ when we reach our neighbour for his own sake, and not when one in need is only the occasion for reaching Christ. The Holy Spirit modifies wholly the notion of partnership. God's Spirit is more than our partner; he is in us.

This is difficult to grasp, and it is even more difficult to comprehend another notion of the Holy Spirit that is common in Catholic theology. Here the Spirit is dynamic, an effective power, and yet in another sense static, identical with what is called "sanctifying grace," with what occurs in baptism, with the lasting power referred to by Jesus in his words "Receive the Holy Spirit to forgive sin." The contemporary Christian may regard all this as a promise, as something which happens ever anew because God keeps his promises, as something that one can rely on and live for, but not as a state of being, a fixed form, a possession or a gurantee. In any case, this presence of the Spirit as vouched for in the Sacrament is not separable but only conceptually distinguishable from his activity in us, from the life lived, from faith and its power.

The Jews suspect abstract speculation or even idolatry in the Christian belief in the Trinity. But Martin Buber speaks of what we confess as the Holy Spirit when he writes about the Eternal in us, the primordial phenomenon of revelation present in the here and now: "The moment of encounter is not an experience that exhausts itself in the elevation of the receptive soul; something happens to the person himself. Sometimes an inspiration, sometimes a struggle; it does not matter what, but something happens. . . . Then man possesses a plus, an increase which he never knew before and whose origin he cannot trace. . . . As the Bible says, those who wait for God are granted power."

No one can object if we wish that this power that comes from God were to be felt by all men, and not only individuals but the whole of mankind, threatened as it is with mass suicide. From this power we hope in peace on earth. We hope in the Spirit of God. From this Spirit we hope for consolation, power, humaneness and holiness for mankind. We believe in *one* God. From *his* Spirit we await for ourselves and for all men that which is beyond our own power.

ALBERT VAN DEN HEUVEL

The holy Catholic (Christian) Church, The Communion of Saints . . .

When I was confirmed in 1950, the massive attack against the church was over. The anti-church atheists had won their hard fight: they were not only recognized as equal and respected citizens, but the leadership of the church in society was a thing of the past. Wherever the atheists were still looked upon as unreliable, deranged, or stupid and wherever the church continued to maintain the façade of the age of Constantine, we knew that it was a question of a remnant condemned to extinction. (And in the fifties, whoever still fought the church was either full of bitterness or an altruistic freedom-fighter who would cast out the unenlightened from his house. Unbelief and belief lived together in peaceful coexistence and engaged in a struggle only when one side tried to limit the freedom of the other. But the campaign against the church had ceased to be a matter of concern.) The church had compromised herself during the war, and her small contingent of martyrs could not save her reputation. The process of secularization had allowed millions of men to leave her and had left faith a private matter, while the modern spirit was estranged from the traditional constructions of dogma and its vocabulary.

Even in the fifties the church was mainly on the defensive, as she had learned during the war. Those who had defended the church against Nazi paganism were called to lead her. Defence of the church and of the orthodox confession had got into their blood, and they continued the struggle against new or newly discovered enemies, against apostasy and against secularization. They dreamed of filling the churches again, and those who had remained faithful were called upon to close ranks. The preachers told us that one man alone cannot be a Christian; we had to visit the church, support her activities, and remember that she was to be visible. Even the ecumenical movement was of help. The church had to become one; the unity which had been lost among various denominations had to be restored. But loyalty to one's own confession came before ecumenical engagement! The Creed had to be defended. Do not let yourselves be led astray by theologians who play their dangerous game far from the real church.

Those of us who entered the church over fifteen years ago were called to work towards renewal. We knew that the church needed renewal, and we knew that the world had become different. A new outlook on life had gradually overpowered us, even though we may not have known what we had to do. Our prophets were those theologians and pastors who spoke of a renewal of lay activity within the *structures*, of youth groups and summer camps, of study clubs for preaching and liturgy, and of work teams for rebuilding demolished churches. We studied the Bible and ignored the great theologians, we organized special services for different classes of workers, and we did many other things. This is the way things went on till the sixties. Though we never spoke of "restoration," but only of renewal, we simply took the traditional structures for granted.

Gradually the church took over this restoration theology. It could easily be integrated into the existing structures, so the initial distrust disappeared. The renewal of activities within the existing church structure became an official slogan, and even today when most church members profess their faith in the one holy church they dream of a church that is largely a thing of the past, a church that runs well, a traditional structure that functions well, large active membership, many activities, large financial contributions. In this sense, the words "I believe in the holy Catholic (Christian) Church; The Communion of Saints" mean that I believe that the Christian church is holy, that is, wholly separate, a society of men who have been called out of the world.

But we soon realized that the restoration did not live up to expectations. We heard, for example, that the Americans complained about the cultural bondage of their church. We in Europe discovered that at best the restoration diminished the exodus from the church but that it did not lead to a new mission. I am fully aware that these remarks are not completely fair. It is true that the restoration did bring many to the faith and did open the eyes of a small group of laymen for realistic and conscious action in the world, but in general not much happened, and that is why the question of church renewal had to be put more sharply than before.

Why must the forms of the church be defended so strongly, since after all they have undergone such change in the course of history? Why are the local congregations of the divided church always referred to as *the* church? How can a community be formed of so many members at the same time? Why must the theologians be the tutors of the laity? Do we really have to spend so much time in church till we are always talking about how much God loves the world? Is it at all possible to prepare oneself theoretically for engagement, or isn't it only through engagement itself that one learns what it means? Is it enough to question the work of the church, or shouldn't we also question her structures? Where are the boundaries of the church—are they connected with the payment of seat-money, or with baptism, or attendance at religious services, or faith, or the imitation of Christ, or the public confession to Christ and his new way of life, or where? What is the church anyway?

This is the real question. What does the church mean? The old answers do not mean much any more: "The church is there where the Word is rightly preached and the Sacraments are properly administered." Precisely! But where is the Word rightly preached and where are the Sacraments properly administered? "The church is where the hierarchy is." The church is surely not a building or an institution. What does the Bible say? This is a good Protestant query, but the answer is far from satisfying: the Scripture only says that the church is many things—people, bride, salt, light. The New Testament employs ninety-six different symbols! This discovery marked the beginning of a theology of renewal: *the church is manifold.* Church means many things at the same time, and this is bound up with the fact that the church cannot be relegated to a corner of our private lives. The church is a new kind of life. Then there was a second discovery: The church is not a place or primarily an institution; *she is an event,* an activity. We do not belong to the church; we are the church. The church is not organized; she is called, she is a way, she happens. This idea is bound up with the fact that God has called the church not for her own sake, but for the sake of the world. And so the third discovery was that the *church is mission.* Mission is not simply one of her many activities, for the church herself is a function of God's mission in the world; she has been called to announce God's good news of hope, of the open future, of the victory over humanity. She is to announce this message, retell it, exemplify it, and keep it alive, just as Jesus did.

The value of church structures depends on whether they serve her mission. The church is holy to the extent that she allows herself to be set apart for mission. She is Christian to the extent that she corrects herself in line with the missionary service of Christ. The church is there where she affects the lives of men who follow Christ. Liturgy, sacraments, sermons, prayers, gatherings—all these are elements of ecclesiastical life, but their sum does not constitute the church. There are no logical demonstrations of the church. We encounter the church only where we observe her missionary service in action. Indeed, this means that the true church is visible, far more visible than we used to think. The church is where men take courage, where there is friendship and readiness for sacrifice, where community arises and where men are free. And even where there are sermons and sacraments, where there are prayers and hymns. There is no church if man is without hope, if he is anxious for the future, or if mutual fear divides the community. It may be a religious gathering, but it is no church.

From all this it is clear that we have to rethink our notions of the relationships between church and denomination and between church and confessional tradition. In my opinion, the denomination or the congregation which is organized along confessional lines is quite impossible as a form of church. To say that one is Catholic, Lutheran, Calvinist or Methodist means very little today. Every church is so divided from within with such inner differentiations that one finds in every church a whole range of variations in Christian belief. Phrases such as "The Catholics believe . . ." or "The Lutherans maintain . . ." are meaningless today. One has to go further and ask: Are you referring to Bea or Ottaviani, Dibelius or Niemoeller, Wilm or Braun?

Involved Christians from all denominations encounter one another today wherever one finds a real discussion of essentials, wherever serious thinking is being done about mission and responsible society. There one finds those Christians who have learned that their traditional confessional language has to be revised, that they need other words not to be found in the tradition-limited vocabulary. The denomination has become for these people an obstacle to renewal, for the denomination belonged to that period when uniformity was necessary for functional efficiency. Today, it is just the opposite! This is the age of unreserved dialogue, and dialogue excludes denomination. This is manifest in the official ecumenical dialogue, where only a very small group of experts participate, and where existing structures exclude the mass. In Europe the denomination rose out of Rome's earlier refusal to reform, to become a church "on the way." The Reformation disregarded the proposal of Erasmus for a gradual renewal within the one church. But now that Rome has become a church "on the way," the whole denominational structure has begun to be radically questioned. During Vatican II we saw how the most varied currents could flow together in "perfect unity" within one church. What is actually left to divide the church? Dogmatic distinctions? But how then do we keep our churches together? Is it not true that only one thing can cause legitimate division within the church: that which prevents the churches from a joint service of the world in life and witness? But if this is true then it has far-reaching consequences.

All these are questions rather than articles of faith. And this is exactly what I understand by faith in the holy church, the communion of saints. For I believe in the church as a continual discussion of faith, as a community which is not limited by the boundaries of any national state but which is always encountering herself visibly on the way. The church has institutions, but this means that she has a membership of those who are not ashamed of the Gospel. They stand up to be counted. But the institution cannot be limited by a form and least of all by a form of denomination. Otherwise we should no longer need to *believe* in the church! Only a bare minimum of structure is needed, only what is required to gather the militia. The most important structural element is universality or catholicity, taken in a quantitative and qualitative sense. Quantitative catholicity embraces the whole world and serves to conquer nationalism, that radical enemy of peace and international justice. Qualitative catholicity embraces the whole revelation and serves to conquer onesidedness, that radical enemy of openness and receptivity. The catholicity of the church is celebrated "locally," whether in the village, the city, the country or the continent. The frequency and the content of that celebration depend on the situation. The existing denominations to which most Christians belong "with or without protest" participate in the church only to the extent that they believe—that is, only to the extent that they manifest that which cannot yet be seen.

MAX-PAUL ENGELMEIER

The Forgiveness of sins . . .

I am a psychiatrist and have been asked to say something about "forgiveness of sins." According to all its methodological statutes, psychiatry regards itself as a modern empirical science. To analyse an article of faith with the instruments of modern science is simply inadmissible, as inadmissible as the chemical analysis of a book. Certainly the chemist can discover many facts about the basic materials, about glue, cellulose, colours, production processes, and so on; about the contents of the book he learns practically nothing. This means that within the experiential range of psychiatry we cannot prove whether or not God forgives sins. Why then have I been asked to reflect on a theme beyond the scope of my science, a theme which escapes my analysis, a theme which calls more questions forth for me than conclusions? I suspect that the reason lies in the great significance of guilt and conscience in psychiatry.

The psychiatrist is forever being asked about guilt and responsibility, about the emotional illness which is expressed as the source of all darkness of the heart and in the world. The scrupulous demand answers as they are driven from one confession of sin to another, mastered by a perverse conscience and incapable of getting to the bottom of their obsession with guilt and reconciliation. Friends and family demand answers as they are deeply injured by pathological outbreaks of shamelessness and hate, of cold disregard and unbridled disgrace. And finally judges demand an expert opinion when they doubt whether a criminal is to be accounted responsible for breaking the law.

People expect that the psychiatrist has something worthwhile to say about guilt, guilt-feelings, and responsibility. And this expectation is well founded, for psychiatry does provide extensive and reliable information about guilt-feelings, their forms, causes, effects, peculiar twists, and pathological variations. And yet I cannot go into all this here, for even a brief outline would exceed the limits of this article, and it would contribute little to the theme "forgiveness of sin."

Martin Buber, to whom we owe much for his clarification of the relationship between existential guilt and guilt-feelings, has shown that there are at least three spheres in which guilt and reconciliation are real. He stresses the fact that the psychiatrist has no competence in the sphere of *law,* where confession, sentence, and indemnification are in question, or in the sphere of *faith,* where it is a matter of the sinner's admission of his guilt before God and his sorrow and his plea for forgiveness. It is another sphere, situated between these two, that concerns the psychiatrist, and he has no competence beyond it. Buber calls this the *sphere of conscience,* and he means that area of human personality where processes occur which have to do with a person's search for meaning: self-enlightenment, self-acceptance, self-surrender.

Buber recognizes this as the sphere of competence assigned to the psychotherapist. In so doing, he shares (though with important reservations) the sober, unmythological notion of conscience common in modern psychiatry. For us, conscience is a central source of personal judgment which man has acquired along with the talent of syntactical speech in the course of his evolution. Ever since man, as distinct from the animal, learned to speak in sentences, he has judged and valued. There are no statements free of judgment and evaluation. Ever since man entered the higher world of speech he has been unable to avoid the question of meaning. And we call conscience the court that questions us inevitably on the significance of each of our actions and of our existence as a whole. Knowledge of the constitution and formative powers of this court are important for understanding our theme. In all phenomena connected with conscience we can distinguish two aspects: one more on the side of feeling, the other more on the side of knowing. When we speak of unrest, anxiety, or the "bite" of conscience, we are talking about the emotional aspect. A discontent which can assume the most varied form, this aspect is experienced very sharply.

Recent research has indicated that such unrest of conscience can occur without the judgment of conscience. This accounts for much anxiety-neurosis and autonomic malfunction. Such patients are not aware of any guilt. Often they are quite sincere when they claim they have done their best to keep the commandments, to lead a decent life and respect the law. And yet, upon closer examination, one finds that they live in a situation that seriously offends their feeling for what is meaningful, proper, and obligatory and their need for uprightness, value, and dignity. If they fail to recognize herein a demand on the part of conscience that incites to a search for and realization of meaningfulness, then the conscience can take the form of an isolated unrest, such as a disturbance in the emotional or autonomic nervous system. The unrest and disturbance usually disappear when the patient realizes that he is really faced with a problem of conscience, that he is justly restless because his freedom to look unconditionally for meaning and to act in a meaningful way is endangered. He recognizes the meaninglessness and absurdity that threaten to turn his existence into the evil of nothingness.

The unrest that pertains to the emotional aspect of conscience is a universal human phenomenon. It occurs whenever a person is threatened with loss of meaning; it is so common that its absence points to a usually serious personality disturbance. An anxiety-reaction in the face of a loss of meaning is a natural characteristic of the normal person. With this uniformity and regularity in the emotional side of the conscience we may contrast the confusing variability and even contradictoriness of that aspect of conscience which lies more on the side of knowledge. For that which we call the judgment of conscience includes such distinct and even opposing elements of meaning that we are tempted to say that there are as many interpretations as there are interpreters.

Since the time of Sigmund Freud we have learned more about the causes of this situation. Today we know that parents transmit to their children the fabric of regulations and norms according to which a particular civilization looks for meaning and tries to realize it. We cannot insist enough on the elementary and biological structure of this process of norm-implantation. It gives a man a system of values that is no more deeply ingrained than the rules of proper table manners. In addition we find in all civilizations among the parents or whoever impresses the norms on the young those who are anxiety-ridden and pedantic, those who are confident and open, and those who are indifferent and phlegmatic. They decide what type of conscience the individual is to have: whether the individual behaves within the world of values as melancholic and scrupulous, free and open, or indifferent.

We cannot deny that mankind as a whole has experienced an evolution of conscience. Our race came from fearful origins: demons in every well and bush; taboos for every place and action; threats, rites, and magic. The numinous was ubiquitous and fearsome; the divinity annihilated both the guilty and the innocent, and no one dared to ask for reasons. In comparison with such religions of taboo, the religions of law were a liberation. Now God formulated law and customs and gave them to this people, who not only kept them but— as the patient Job—could plead their own case before God. Within the limits of the sacred law, man became a partner of a lawgiver who established meaning. Most men today have a conscience that still corresponds to this religion of law. Only very few are capable of matching the giant step of Jesus of Nazareth who fulfilled the law by illuminating its meaning: the openness and freedom of love.

The churches are seldom happy with these rare individuals, yet this evolution which I have indicated as an aspect of the historical development of mankind is precisely the great task facing man in this time of transition to a planetary, technological civilization. Most people manage to go somewhat beyond the stage of infantile anxiety, taboo, and rite. Schools, churches, and jobs help man to transform his childish need for security and meaning into the norms and laws of a realistic structure. But this transformation, which marks the end of puberty, is for the majority the last stage reached by conscience. Yet every day in our contacts with the truth, with money, with our job, our colleagues, our sexuality, and our automobile, we are driven to search anew for meaning. Is it really meaningful, the way I live with my wife and children, the way I behave on the street and in the city? A superstitious timidity and often a deep-rooted anxiety prevent many from frankly posing such questions and from not seeking refuge behind the misunderstood Ten Commandments or isolated passages from the Scriptures. Many Philistines employ the same device when they try to check their fear of the logical question of meaning by resorting to the moral vocabulary of the libertine, the materialist, or the indifferent atheist.

In fact the psychiatrist, whose task it is to encourage man in the free search for and realization of meaning, knows that this maturity must be paid for with anxiety. For there comes a time when he who has become mature sees his questions for meaning lose themselves in darkness, so that the learned answers have no longer the power of exorcism, and there is no absolute and always valid answer at all. Not to deviate, not to hide, but to enter questioningly this darkness as if one were going to meet a beloved Thou—this is how the man of free and mature conscience seeks for meaning.

The psychiatrist can go no further. But neither can he exclude what Martin Buber confessed when he wrote: "... whoever speaks the word 'God' and really means 'Thou' addresses the true Thou of his life, no matter what illusion may hold him captive. He addresses a Thou that cannot be limited by any other and in his relation to that Thou he embraces all others. But even he who despises the Name and professes to be godless, if he addresses the Thou of his life with the whole of his offered nature, a Thou that cannot be limited by any other, he too addresses God."

Will the Thou, sought in darkness and confusion and with the surrender of one's whole being, leave the searcher in his confusion, darkness, and lostness? Will the Thou manifest itself as the reconciling goal of the search, as the meaning of the surrender? I end with this question and with the admission that I believe it better to dare to search for an ultimate, all-embracing meaning than to save oneself, protected by shells emptied of meaning, for a sterile nothingness.

MAX SECKLER

The Resurrection of the body . . .

The story is told of a theology professor who had been a credit to his profession and who had reached the age of retirement, so that he finally had time to study questions of special interest to him personally. He began to examine the problems of death and the hereafter, though this had never been his area of specialization. So he started to collect all possible books and learned monographs on the subject. Because he was old and death stood before him, it was not a question of distant curiosity; he had to find out what lay before him before he went off on the journey of no return. For years he studied perseveringly, patiently, and yet with growing impatience. Finally he threw his books away in despair and explained: "One knows nothing on the subject! Unknowing and blind, I have to take the last step."

This story is not imaginary. I know the name of this man, who died a difficult but good death. He was a believing Christian, a professor of theology, and so an expert in matters of faith, and during his life he had held fast to the Creed in which we read "I believe in the Resurrection of the body." His attempt to examine the basis of this hope and to illumine his faith with knowledge failed. I must confess that I was moved when I heard the story and when I thought of his situation. But when I recently began to check the literature to discover just what the church and her theology had to say about this subject, then I experienced the same as he. I must add that this feeling is rather widespread today and even manifests itself in the literature itself. The optimism of earlier times, the old certainty of our knowledge about the hereafter is gone. The perplexed helplessness of theology is most evident in this area of "the last things." This is understandable and even obvious, for human speech must become a stutter when it reaches the boundaries of this world of space-time.

But this was not always the case. There were times when man thought he knew the exact structure of the world with its underworld and heaven and when the ancient physics and topography could assimilate all theories. The textbooks were full of learned hypotheses. Man knew, for example, what the hereafter looked like and what went on there. It was especially in regard to the resurrection of the body that man had formed detailed descriptions of the risen body and its activities: whether one could eat and drink, whether the digestive system still worked, whether the distinction of sex still held, and so on. Man thought that he understood how the soul repossessed a body long distintegrated into dust and how God reunited the elements and revivified the dead skeleton. I have even run across the theory that the bodies of all the risen would assume the age of thirty years and would be of male sex. The highest ideal of this pious adventurer was obviously that of a thirty-year-old male hero.

In view of all this earlier speculation, we ask how man regards the profession of belief in the resurrection of the body today. What is certain is that the last things—man's death, resurrection, and otherworldly fate—are no longer subject to description. The whole notion of the universe has changed. The imaginary world of the resurrection no longer exists; where heaven used to be, human astronauts and not angelic beings are wandering in space. God has been robbed of his heaven, and according to our human mode of thinking he has become homeless. We can no longer assign heaven to a place and can no longer imagine that countless billions of transfigured human bodies are to be walking some day through the universe.

And what about our traditional faith? It would seem to be in a desperate plight, which is worsened when we act as if nothing has changed. One way out seems to be the reduction of the ancient hope in heaven to hope in the earth and in the hands of the scientist and physician who are to assure eternal life. Whoever dies too soon can be put in deep freeze for better days. Accordingly, a better future would become our

God and our heaven, and man himself would be able to sketch its outline on his drawing-boards.

I am not sure, but I suspect that this latter-day speculation will eventually be subject to as much ridicule as is that of traditional theology with its detailed account of the hereafter. Man is by nature an impatient being; nothing annoys him more than having to restrain his impatient imagination. He restlessly makes plans for new and better worlds, and the builders of the future have already convinced us of the soundness of their projects. And yet, here is a basic misunderstanding. I am not thinking of the consolation of a faith that everything will turn out right after all, but of the illusionary expectation that man himself can assure his own happiness. If there is a God, then mortal man can find his salvation only in him, and this is why we have to rethink our faith in the resurrection of the body.

To shed a little light on this teaching we must begin by finding out exactly what is meant by this article of the Creed. If we trace the history of the statement regarding the resurrection of the body back to its origins, we are surprised to find that it had a difficult time of it and that it caused much misunderstanding. In its present form we do not find it in the Scriptures. The formula was first used by the Christian communities of the first century to express their belief in the resurrection. The usage goes back to scriptural origins inasmuch as "body" in the Scriptures refers to the whole man—not only to his physical body but to the whole man in his corporeal reality. As long as men realized that "resurrection of the body" really meant "resurrection of man" in every aspect of his existence, there was no problem, at least regarding the formula of expression. It was only later, after man had learned to distinguish soul from body (an immortal soul at that), that the real problem began and led to endless speculation about the reanimation of human corpses. On this subject the Creed has nothing to say. It would have been much better to have spoken only about the resurrection of man to eternal life.

Another difficulty is the inimical attitude to the body held by many philosophies and religions. For those who look upon the body as the prison of the soul, redemption can only mean liberation from the body. If man is an unhappy combination of soul and body, of angel and animal, then he has the obligation, as Schiller says, to renounce "the lusts of the worm" and "Stand as an angel before God." But the Bible, on the contrary, proclaims the salvation of man as a whole: not a redemption *from* the body, but the salvation of the entire man, characterized as he is by corporeality. The formula "resurrection of the body," though it has led to the misunderstandings mentioned above, does offer protection against those who despise the body.

Misunderstandings are always with us, but they shouldn't prevent us from getting to the heart of the matter. The whole point of this creedal statement is that man as a whole, in his corporeal and historical reality, is the object of salvation. Corporeality is not merely a temporary quality of man; it is an ultimate determination whereby "corporeality" does not refer to a coagulation of matter but to a form of human existence. This means that when I say, "I believe in the Resurrection of the body," I confess that nothing of what I have done and experienced during my earthly stay is to be annihilated. What is to be saved is not a neutral, indifferent, and undifferentiated immortal soul; I myself and all of what I am have received the promise of eternal life.

We cannot explore further this promise and the hope that it gives. All further speculation and every attempt to lift the veil of mystery and to describe the "how" of it is useless. We may stutter and stumble when we try to justify this final and decisive hope, but it alone is able to keep us from despising life or regarding it as a nonsensical circus; life becomes for us the workroom in which we find and build up the elements of eternal life. Our hope is not subject to scientific proof or disproof, but it does have a convincing basis: the witness of the New Testament to the resurrection of Jesus. The men of the New Testament were not dreamers, and we know that in spite of all they looked upon death with horror. They did not minimize the necessity of dying, blinded by the beauty of their hope. They could look death in the face, for they knew that the end was not nothingness or a realm of nameless shadows, but man as loved, accepted, and raised up by God.

GERHARD EBELING

And the Life everlasting

Eternal life is unquestionably a matter of faith. Yet we can scarcely believe in something that wholly escapes our rational thought. How is it possible to think about eternal life?

Doesn't this question put us on the wrong track? You will object: "Like everything else that is a matter of faith, the notion of eternal life surely surpasses human thought even if it doesn't simply contradict it." In the interest of this faith, such an objection must be answered, for the genuine and inevitable contradiction which faith raises to the claim of disbelief is not the blind and senseless contradiction raised by superstition.

Faith in eternal life does indeed allow us to use our minds, and we are inclined first of all to think of the contrary against which such a faith is directed. In matters of faith, we must be prepared to accept war, to suffer contradiction, and to offer defence. If there be an eternal life, surely it is one of eternal peace and happiness. And yet, our faith in this eternal life is not without contradiction and struggle. In fact, more than any other article of the Creed, this last article incites challenge and demands argument.

We need not look very far to find its contrary. We see it all around us in a very concrete form. We are mortal, and the motive forces of our life are ephemeral and perishable: our hungers and delights, our anxieties and joys, our works and possessions, our loves and disappointments, our plans and hopes. Whoever confesses his belief in eternal life must look at life openly and honestly as he really observes and experiences it. He must believe in the face of everything that carries within itself the seeds of death. And who can escape this evident contradiction? What is there that does not oppose it?

We need only think of the graves that have buried a part of our lives: our mother, our father, a friend, a son or daughter. We need only regard our own body with its recognized and more often unrecognized traces of age and decay. We may also think of whatever mercifully hides and permits us to forget the bitter end: our short-lived and thereby eternally hungering lust for life. To think of such things is to break through the illusion; it does not destroy it, but it forces us to recognize its limits and conditions.

We do not have to limit our sight to our own private interests. We can see the million-fold life, suffering, and death around us, levelled in the universal web of fate and yet objects of the individual experience which each must endure for himself. We see the endless stream of generations and peoples before us, swept forward in the vortex of history and cast into the whirlpool of the past centuries that are but instants in the space-time of the universe.

And so it goes on, and no one knows how or how long. Certainly not for eternity. Our life-expectation may increase somewhat, as it has in the last decades. The art of outwitting death will surely advance in equal tread with the art of delivering to death a mass harvest. The growing talent of manipulating and hoarding life and death may displace the line between them; it cannot separate them forever. Life will remain a life in time and directed to death. It would be absurd and even horrifying to imagine that human life be extended without limit in time. Death is usually regarded as the threat to life's meaning. But if the boundary between life and death were to disappear, would not then life's meaning be really lost for good? Wouldn't everything then be indifferent and pale, a limitless long-suffering?

In the harsh, synthetic light of science and technology, we are able to see some things more clearly than our fathers did. When they spoke of eternal life, they may have been more aware of the night and seriousness of death than we who have banished the thought from our consciousness or who regard it as a matter for sensational reading. Nevertheless, they were able to contradict death by thinking of a life without death. We, on the contrary, are used to regarding death and life as purely biological phenomena. In medical-pharmaceutical discussion on life and death, we have gained ground. But it seems altogether meaningless to oppose death radically if we accept it as a biological fact. For in this case life and death are merely aspects of one single process, and "eternal life" is a self-contradiction. Can we imagine life without intrinsic movement and change, without privation and imperfection? Does not the idea of total satisfaction and eternal blessedness destroy the notion of life? Wouldn't life cease if there were nothing more to be gained, if no more ups and downs were in view?

Surely, our elders knew that it is a language of imagery that speaks of eternal life as of a paradisal existence, a joyous feast, a heavenly song of praise, a vision of God's glory. But, for them, these images breathed reality, whereas for us the chasm between image and reality has widened enormously. A lack of imagery threatens to reduce belief in eternal life to speechlessness, and speechlessness threatens to bring the end of faith. The thought of eternity has become alien to our time. And this affects not only the very last article of the Christian profession of faith but the whole of faith itself.

But we have no right to call a halt there, as if there were nothing more to be said. Have we really a proper notion of the contradiction that inevitably accompanies a belief in eternal life? Most difficulties in faith are caused today by confused thinking. It is true that the real root of opposition to faith is not a matter of intellect but of a radical aversion of will, which may be camouflaged by intellectual problems, especially those resulting from a deficient and inadequate form of thinking. Poor thinking obscures faith and puts the unbeliever in the right. It shifts the battle to the wrong front and dulls the edge of attack. The salt loses its savour and is rightly trampled by the masses. The real scandal of the faith is that its confession of eternal life clearly contradicts a life that will not hear of eternity.

What is eternity? It clearly implies an opposition to time. But in what sense? In the sense that it denies any limitation of time? If we do not choose our words carefully, we get into the habit of speaking this way. We complain of an indeterminate period of waiting: "It lasted an eternity," though this eternity lasted only ten minutes. Nor does even an infinite progression of time constitute eternity. Is then eternity the absolute negation of time, a timelessness? We talk about eternal truths and refer to universal verities that are indifferent to time, such as the statement about the sum of angles in a triangle. But this is not the biblical meaning of eternity.

When God, as the living God, is called "eternal," thereby linking the ideas of eternity and life, this is not at all an expression of indifference to time. On the contrary, it implies a relation of intense involvement in time. But we must not use here the formalized and neutral idea of measurable time. Eternity is not an idea from physics; it is a religious idea. If we confuse the religious idea with the narrow concept of physical time, we can only end in ridiculous and imaginary problems, such as have caused unnecessary trouble to piety and theology in the area of "the last things."

We have to begin with our relation to time. Man never has enough time; he lives under the pressure of time. This is not the case for the plant or animal, however much they are bound by time. They are in time immediately and without their consent, while man is aware of time and thereby becomes a problem to himself. He is addicted to the past and rushes into the future, full of fantasies about things that are not present to him. He is not in harmony with his present. He remembers and plans, he worries himself with guilt-feelings and cares, carrying the burden of a growing past and a diminishing future. Whether, driven by activism or lust for life, he has not enough time, or whether he kills time, not knowing where to begin, he is in either case not one with his time and therefore not one with himself. More than all temporal things, man is deeply affected by time. Man's relation to time affects whatever makes him human—his reason, conscience, and speech—as well as whatever makes him fail and abuse his humanity. He wants to be lord over his time, and this makes him ever more subject to it.

God is the Lord of time. Eternity is his divine power over time, the unlimited freedom to apportion time and to end it. Eternity and time are not disparate entities that cancel one another; at a profound level they are complementary. Time is the utterance of eternity; eternity is the mystery of time. They belong together like creator and creation. This means that the intelligibility of eternity embraces two elements: the divinity of God and the humanity of man.

Eternal life belongs properly to God alone. That we can believe in God as Spirit and as love explains why eternal life is no contradiction. The Spirit that gives life and the love that has no end do not acquiesce in man's distortion of faith in the Creator into a pseudo-scientific theory of the origin of world, time, and life. Spirit and love point to the life that is the core of temporal life and that makes man whole when he has it. That eternal life belongs to God alone, does not contradict but emphasizes the fact that man does not possess it in and of himself. His salvation is not his own; it comes when he loses himself and gives himself to the Spirit and love of the promise.

Faith in eternal life, therefore, has its true counterpart in the life we live and not in the death that ends it. Faith in eternal life stands in absolute contradiction to a life closed upon itself, a life that grasps for time through works or pleasure, through cares or dissipation, and thereby grants death its power. Faith in eternal life is no play of imagination about man's condition after death, so that he can disarm death. This faith means taking God seriously as Lord of life.

As far as God's lordship goes, for Christians it is consummated in Jesus, whom they confess to God's honour as the Lord of life and death. This fact determines our thinking about eternal life. It is neither a substitute for nor a prolongation of this life after death. It is rather the conquest and fulfilment of this life through death. There is another life than that which ends in death. There is the freedom from death, its fulfilment and conquest. The Cross of Jesus teaches us how to regard eternal life: it is the life in which we now share through faith in him, the new life of courage for the temporal, courage to accept and to surrender all things in praise of him. Who believes in the Son has eternal life, we read in John's Gospel. For wherever there is forgiveness of sins there is also life and beatitude, as Luther teaches in his Catechism.

It is wholly in line with faith in Jesus that we no longer

think of eternal life by means of images: a spatial heaven above the earth and a temporal extension after death. The truth of what is called "heaven" and "after death" has to be released from the bonds of our scientific notions of space-time. If one should regret this and complain that thereby faith becomes still more obscure, we may ask whether this is not precisely the way of faith: to walk in darkness in the certainty that it is not darkness for God nor for him who expects in death only God and nothing more.

The nonperceptual character of faith in eternal life forces us back to the experience from which this faith originates: the unconditional and decisive claims and accusations of our conscience in this temporal life, and its unconditional and decisive liberation and certitude through the word of eternal life. This dual experience is inseparable from death. It deepens the seriousness of this life, and through it the joy of eternal life is purified and fulfils itself in spite of everything.